To Didi with all my Love, York 2nd. Oct. 1990

Shally.
xxx

A HISTORY OF YORKSHIRE

THE DARWEN COUNTY HISTORY SERIES

A History of Yorkshire

F. B. SINGLETON and S. RAWNSLEY

Drawings by Keith Woodcock

Cartography by G. Bryant and R. Fry

PHILLIMORE

1986

Published by
PHILLIMORE & CO. LTD.
Shopwyke Hall, Chichester, Sussex

ISBN 0 85033 619 8

Printed and bound in Great Britain by
Biddles Ltd, Guildford and King's Lynn

Contents

Maps

List of Plates

Acknowledgements

The courtesy of the following for permission to publish illustrations is gratefully acknowledged by the authors: Peter Wilkes, nos. 1, 9, 22; Clifford Robinson, nos. 2-6, 10, 14, 16, 20, 21, 23, 26-28, 30, 31, 33, 34, 37, 38, 46, 47, 49, 50; Mr. P. Walsham, no. 9; Geoffrey N. Wright, no. 12; The National Trust, nos. 17, 18; R. Oddy, nos. 24, 25; Tim Smith (BHRU), no. 29; W. R. Mitchell, no. 32; N. Buckly, no. 35; Varley Picture Agency, nos. 36, 41, 51, 52; National Portrait Gallery, London, nos. 42-45.

Preface

This book is based on one written by F. Singleton and the late W. E. Tate, and first published by Darwen Finlayson in 1960. The present volume is in many ways a new book, although the basic framework of the original version has been retained. The text, however, has been greatly expanded, more maps and photographs have been added, and a new feature is the inclusion of line drawings in the margins of each page. New chapters on Yorkshire after the Industrial Revolution and on Yorkshire's cultural achievements have been added by Dr Stuart Rawnsley, who in addition is particularly responsible for chapters XIII, XIV, XV, XVI and XVII.

Since the first edition there has been a major reorganisation of the boundaries of Yorkshire, and the county which appears on the administrative map of the 1980s is very different from that of the 1960s. However, the county which lies in the hearts and minds of most Yorkshire people, and which existed on the map for the millennium before the boundary changes of 1974, has not changed. As historians, we therefore regard it as justifiable that the present book should be mainly about the Yorkshire of the three Ridings, although due attention has been paid to the changes of the recent past.

Even considering the enlarged format we feel it necessary to echo the opening words of the first edition in recognising that we have attempted a difficult undertaking 'in trying to compress the story of Yorkshire, even in outline, within the limits of so short a book. Clearly we had to be highly selective, and to omit much which we would gladly have included'. The choices which we have had to make may not be to the taste of all our readers, but we hope that what follows will offer a readable, interesting and well balanced portrait of a great county. We should be happy to receive from readers any suggestions for improvements, and any corrections which they may find necessary. We have consulted others and received helpful suggestions. In particular we would like to thank Mr. David Joy and Mr. Jack Reynolds for their valuable assistance. But we are, of course, responsible for any errors which might have crept in.

Fred Singleton
Stuart Rawnsley

The late W. E. Tate, B.Litt., F.S.A.

Bill Tate, who was co-author of the first edition of this book, died in 1968, his last published work being *The English Village Community and the Enclosure Movement*. Tate's reputation as a local historian is based primarily on his classic work *The Parish Chest* (1946), which is still the standard work on parish records; and on his *Domesday of English Enclosure Acts and Awards* (1978). He was an original – and in the nicest sense a mildly eccentric – scholar, and a born teacher, whose influence on his students, many of whom are now teachers of history in Yorkshire schools and universities, is still remembered with affection and respect. Although the present book is in many ways different from the first edition – it is twice as long and has many more illustrations – its basic plan is that laid down by Tate a quarter of a century ago. There are a few pages of his original text which remain, but above all, I hope, as Tate's pupil and collaborator, that the lively style, the scholarship, and something of the spirit of Bill Tate survives in the present volume.

Fred Singleton

I Physical Geography

The influence of geography can be traced in many aspects of the life of the county of Yorkshire and this is why a book which is primarily concerned with Yorkshire history must begin by introducing the reader to some of the main physical features of the stage on which the historical events have taken place.

The Yorkshire which is the subject of this book, 'the county of broad acres', is still the largest geographical county in England and Wales, despite the territorial losses incurred as a result of the 1974 administrative reorganisation. In the form which it held for the millennium before 1974 it covered almost four million acres, and at the last census before 1974 it was the home of over five million people (for present area and population, see table on page 122). The West Riding was the largest administrative county in England and Wales, but since 1974 the new North Yorkshire County Council now governs a larger area than any other county council in England and Wales.

At its greatest north-south extent the geographical county stretches for about eighty miles, and at its widest point it covers about a hundred miles, from Flamborough Head to the Lancashire border. Its 100-mile long coastline reaches south from the estuary of the Tees to the Humber at Spurn Point; and on the west it comes in places to within ten miles of the coast at Morecambe Bay.

There are five broad geographical divisions. The Pennines, which occupy the western third of the county, are themselves divided in two by the Craven lowlands, an area bounded by lines of geological disturbance, known as the Craven Faults. To the south the predominant surface rock is millstone grit, a coarse sandstone which carries a cover of peat bog, heather and cotton grass. To the north, and especially in the area known to physical geographers as the Askrigg Block, limestones predominate and give rise to such dramatic scenic features as Malham Cove, Kilnsey Crag and Giggleswick Scar. The limestone, which is partly soluble in weakly acidic rainwater, has been eroded by underground streams to produce caves and subterranean valleys, which are a great attraction to cavers and potholers. Some of the caves, like Victoria Cave above the town of Settle, and Kinsey and Kelcow Caves near Giggleswick Scar, were at times the home of prehistoric inhabitants of Yorkshire.

In some places between the Craven lowlands and Swaledale, another

Brimham Rocks: wind eroded sandstone

geological formation is to be found. This is the so-called Yoredale series (Yoredale=Uredale=Wensleydale), which consists of alternating layers of limestones, and sandstones and shales, lying between the great scar limestone and the grit. The difference in resistance to erosion of the rocks in this formation gives rise to the stepped effect to be seen on the sides of some of the Pennine valleys, in Upper Wharfedale, Wensleydale and Swaledale. The term Carboniferous is used to distinguish the main Pennine geological formations from the earlier rocks which underlie them – like, for example, the Silurian which are exposed near Ingleton and the Ordovician at Horton in Ribblesdale – and the newer glacial deposits which lie on top of them, such as the drumlin field at Ribblehead and the glacial erratics at Norber. This is because above the gritstone there was originally a series of rocks known as the Coal Measures (i.e. Carboniferous), which contained seams of local coal interspersed with shales, sandstones and other rocks. Although coal seams do occur in other formations, they are most abundant in the Coal Measures. The only place in the mid-Pennines where the Coal Measures survive today is in the Ingleton area, where coal was worked until about the time of the First World War, but Coal Measures are to be found in abundance on the flanks of the Pennines, especially on the eastern side, southward from the Leeds-Bradford-Selby line; and across the borders into Nottinghamshire and Derbyshire. The most famous summits in the Yorkshire Pennines are the Three Peaks (Pen-y-ghent, Ingleborough and Whernside), but the highest point in the county is Micklefell (2,591 ft.). South of the Craven lowlands the peaks are lower, the highest point in the southern region being Black Hill (1,908 ft.) on the Derbyshire border, near the Holme Moss television station.

The second great geographical division of Yorkshire is the Vale of York, which runs through the centre of the county from Durham to the Nottinghamshire-Derbyshire border. It is drained mainly by the river Ouse and its tributaries, although a northern extension, passing through the Vale of Mowbray, reaches into Teesdale. In its southern extremity it touches the fenlands at the head of the Humber estuary and the low lying peat moors around Thorne and Hatfield. The Vale of York, at the centre of which lies the city of York, contains some of the richest arable land in Britain, although there are some areas of infertile sands and gravels, and others which are subject to flooding. Along the western edge of the Vale runs a narrow belt of magnesian limestone, part of which is followed by the Great North Road (A1). The characteristic building stone which is quarried from this formation can be seen in churches, houses and public buildings in Tadcaster, Barwick-in-Elmet and Pontefract.

The Vale of York separates the Pennines from the uplands in the eastern half of Yorkshire – the North York Moors, the Howardian Hills and the Yorkshire Wolds. The North York Moors, which reach their highest point at Urra Moor (1,490 ft.), consist mainly of sandstones and

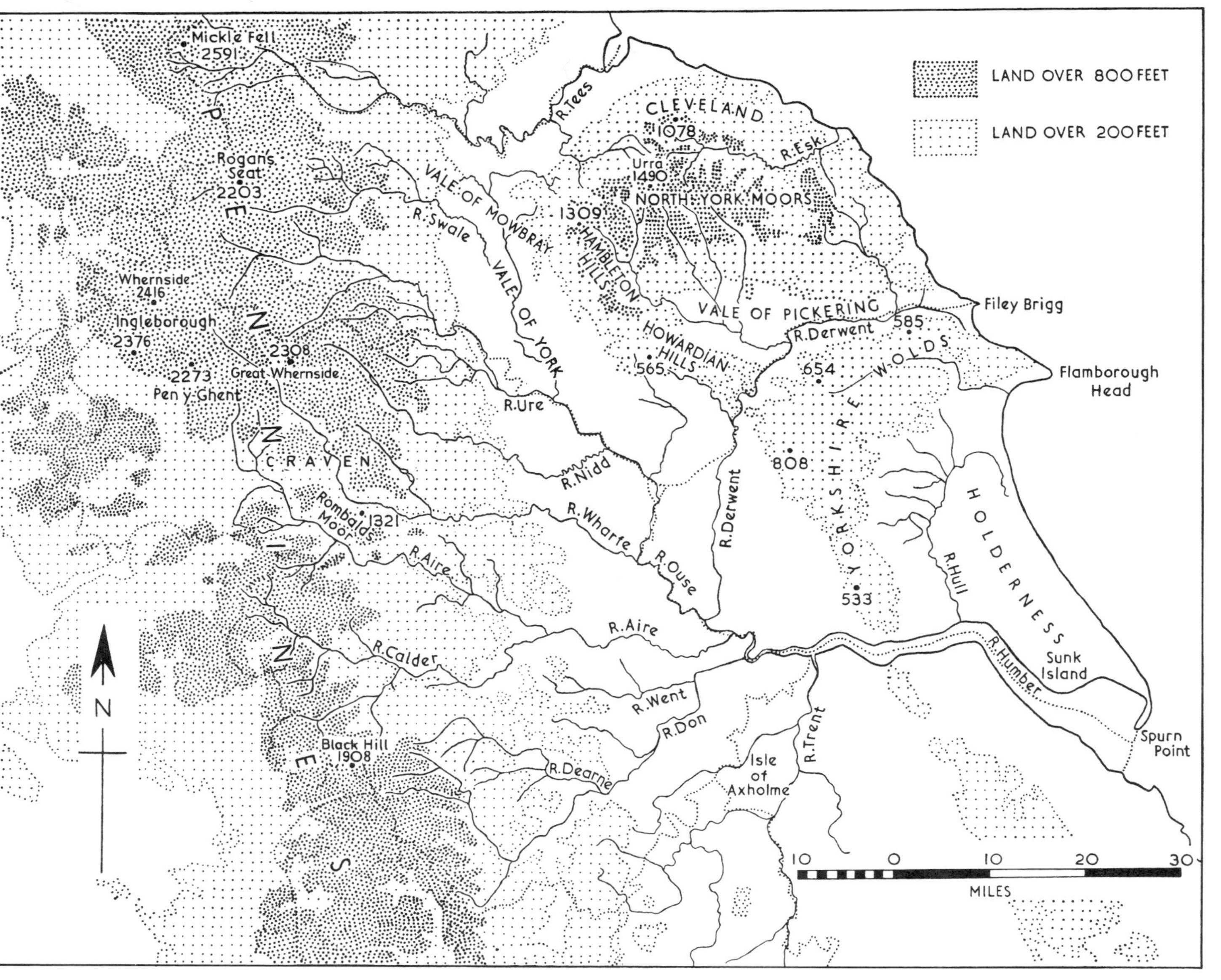

Map 1. Physical Map of Yorkshire.

limestones of Jurassic age, which are more recent in geological time than are the Carboniferous rocks of the Pennines. The oolitic limestone of the Cleveland area contains bands of iron ore which have provided the raw material for the iron and steel industry of Teesside. The Howardian Hills, which run across the western end of the Vale of Pickering between Malton and Ampleforth, are composed of Jurassic rock of similar age to those of the North York Moors. In their foothills Vanbrugh's magnificent 18th-century country house, Castle Howard, is to be found. The river Derwent, which flows across the Vale of Pickering, breaks through the Howardian Hills in a gorge which is the present day manifestation of the overflow channel which drained Lake Pickering, a glacial lake which occupied the floor of the Vale during the last Ice Age.

The Vale of Pickering, drained by the river Derwent and its tributaries, separates the North York Moors from the chalk hills of the Yorkshire Wolds, which form a crescent-shaped arc enfolding the former East Riding. The Wolds meet the sea at the spectacular white cliffs of Flamborough Head. West of Hull, near Hessle, they cross the Humber near the site of the new Humber Bridge, the northern anchorage of which is founded in the chalk at a depth of 21m. The chalk formation continues south of the river as the Lincolnshire Wolds. The steep slopes of the Wolds escarpment, which face the Vales of Pickering and York, are in contrast to the more gentle east- and south-facing slopes which descend to the valley of the river Hull, and the Plain of Holderness.

Memorial to the Yorkshire geologist, Adam Sedgwick, in Dent, North Yorkshire

The Plain of Holderness, which lies between the river Hull and the North Sea, is composed mainly of boulder clay, a substance of glacial origin which dates from the last Ice Age. Although it produces rich agricultural land in suitable circumstances, it also contains less fertile areas, and some which are badly drained. The largest lake in East Yorkshire, Hornsea Mere, lies close to the coast, in the clay of Holderness. The cliffs along the North Sea coast between Flamborough Head and the Humber are also of boulder clay, which is soft and easily eroded by the sea (see below, Chapter XXI).

Four-fifths of Yorkshire is drained by rivers which enter the Humber, most by way of the Ouse and its tributaries. A small part of the Western Pennines drains by the Ribble to the Irish Sea, and there are some streams which flow from the North York Moors directly into the North Sea. The lower courses of the main rivers are navigable for small boats, and in the early history of the county these waterways, supplemented by canals built in the 18th and 19th centuries, played an important part in the commercial and industrial life of the people.

II Prehistoric Yorkshire

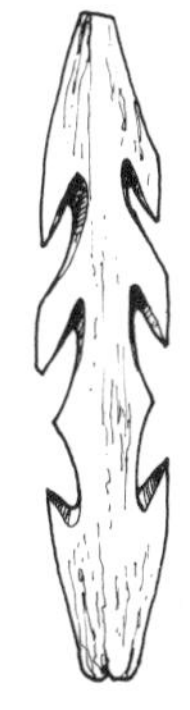

Bone harpoon, Victoria Cave

About 10,000 years ago, at the end of the last Ice Age, the first humans entered Yorkshire, in the wake of the shrinking ice cap which had previously covered northern England. At that time the appearance of the land differed greatly from that which we see today. There was a land connection with continental Europe, across the area of the southern half of the North Sea, making it possible for groups of Stone Age hunters to wander from North Germany and Jutland to Eastern England, in search of food and shelter. Their food came from wild animals, birds and fish which they caught and killed; and from wild berries and fruits which they collected. Their shelter was often in caves, such as Victoria Cave above Settle and Kirkdale Cave near Pickering. There is evidence that these caves have revealed the remains of animals which flourished during the last inter-glacial period, when there was a warm, sub-tropical climate. The hyaenas had dragged into their caves the carcases and bones of lions, elephants, rhinoceros and hippopotami. The so-called 'Leeds hippopotamus', found by workmen in a clay pit at Wortley in 1854 – and which they took to a local museum curator because they thought they were too large to be 'Christians' bones' – were in fact the remains of three animals. These bones can still be seen in the Leeds City Museum. When the first people came, however, the climate was sub-arctic, and the animals which the Old Stone Age (or Palaeolithic) hunters found were mammoth, woolly rhinoceros and reindeer. One Palaeolithic group settled at Starr Carr, near Scarborough, living in tents made from animal skins, which were erected on wooden platforms around the edge of the ice-dammed Lake Pickering. Another site occupied by these Maglemosian fisherfolk and hunters was at Flixton, under the scarp of the Wolds, a few miles west of Filey.

During the 5,000 years following the arrival of these first migrants the climate steadily improved, and a richer natural vegetation began to cover the land. The birch was one of the first species of trees to appear, followed by hazel, pine, elm, oak and alder. There were changes in the relationship between land and sea, as the evidence of old shore lines bears witness. At one time Holderness was covered by sea and a shore line ran along the eastern slopes of the Wolds. By 5,000 B.C. the separation of Britain from mainland Europe had occurred, and later arrivals had to cross the Channel or North Sea in dugout canoes. The remains of ancient forests are sometimes dredged up from the bed of the North Sea.

Flint arrowhead, Grimston

Several phases of Stone Age culture are presented in Yorkshire, and tools and weapons made of stone, bone, antler – and even of a boar's tusk – may be seen in museums throughout the county.

Tiny worked flints – known as pygmy flints – can still be found in parts of the Pennines. These were created by people of the Middle Stone (Mesolithic) Age, who are known as Tardenoisians, after a district in Belgium, where archaeologists first identified this culture. Another Mesolithic group, the Azilians, occupied parts of the Craven district in the sixth millennium B.C. Implements from these Mesolithic cultures are to be found in the Pig Yard Museum at Settle and in the museums in Skipton and Grassington. Mesolithic flints have also been found in Stump Cross Caverns, between Grassington and Pateley Bridge.

Around 3,000 B.C. a revolutionary advance was made in the cultural development of the area, with the arrival from the continent of the first Neolithic (or New Stone Age) settlers. As the North Sea and the English Channel had by this time assumed approximately their present outlines, these people must have crossed in boats – probably dugout canoes. The so-called 'Neolithic Revolution' involved arable farming and the domestication of animals. Neolithic society knew how to make pottery, weave cloth and make baskets. It was no longer necessary to live a semi-nomadic existence. Permanent settlements were built, like the one at Ulrome, between Hornsea and Bridlington, where a dwelling built on wooden piles on the shore of a shallow lake has been discovered. Under the platform were found the bones of domestic animals – horses, pigs, dogs and sheep – as well as those of wild animals like wolves, boar and beavers. The Neolithic folk buried their dead with some ceremony, in chambered mounds known as barrows. There are examples in Yorkshire of both long and round barrows. In some there are signs that cremation was practised. At Duggleby Howe, near Wharram-le-Street, there is a large round barrow, 20 ft. high – the largest of its kind in Britain – where a mass cremation appears to have taken place. A similar structure is to be found at Willy Howe, 10 miles to the east. Neolithic barrows are found in many places in the Wolds, for example, at Willerby near Filey; and at Hedon House near Burythorpe. The evidence of burial rituals associated with the barrows suggests that the Neolithic peoples had some religious beliefs, and probably believed in a life after death.

Standing stone, Rudston

Some of the most impressive prehistoric monuments are associated with a group of invaders who arrived about 2,000 B.C. They are known as the Megalith builders, from the large standing stones which they erected, presumably for ceremonial purposes, probably connected with some form of religion. The Devil's Arrows, a group of three pillars of millstone grit, each standing about 20 ft. high and buried to a depth of five feet, stand in a field near Boroughbridge. There were, originally, several other stones in the group. The stone is thought to have been transported from a quarry near Knaresborough, over six miles away.

1. Multangular Tower, York. A ten-sided tower in the Roman walls of York, built in the 4th century A.D.

2. St Gregory's 'Little Minster', Kirkdale. The Minster is of Anglo-Saxon origins. The sundial over the door dates from 1060 and refers to Earl Tostig.

3. (*above*) Goodmanham church, East Yorkshire. This church stands on the site of a pagan temple which was destroyed by the pagan priest, Coifi, after he had accepted Christianity around A.D. 627. To commemorate this there is a stained glass window showing Coifi with the broken idols of the pagan faith at his feet.

4. (*below*) Norman crypt, Lastingham, dating from 1080, on the site of a monastery church dedicated to St Cedd, built in A.D. 654 and destroyed by the Danes.

5. The Norman church of St Nicholas at Askham Bryan, near York.

6. The beautiful double arches of the Norman church at Riccall, near York. The church was built about 1160, but modified in the 15th century.

Domesday Book is, of course, in Latin, but the reader having no Latin may quite easily make out much of the general sense of many of the entries. Thus, in the extract below, *EURVICSCIRE* is YORKSHIRE, and the rest of the heading reads: LANDS OF ILBERT DE LACY, WEST RIDING, SKYRACK WAPENTAKE (see p. 17). The last entry shown reads:

4 MANORS — In *THORNER* had Ulchil, Uluer, Berguluer & Ulstan 8 ploughlands (assessed) to the geld, & 4 ploughs may be there. Now Ilbert has there 2 villeins & 1 bordar with 2 ploughs. (There is) wood (land) pasturable half a league in length and as much in breadth. T.R.E. it was worth 4 pounds, now (it is worth) 10 shillings.

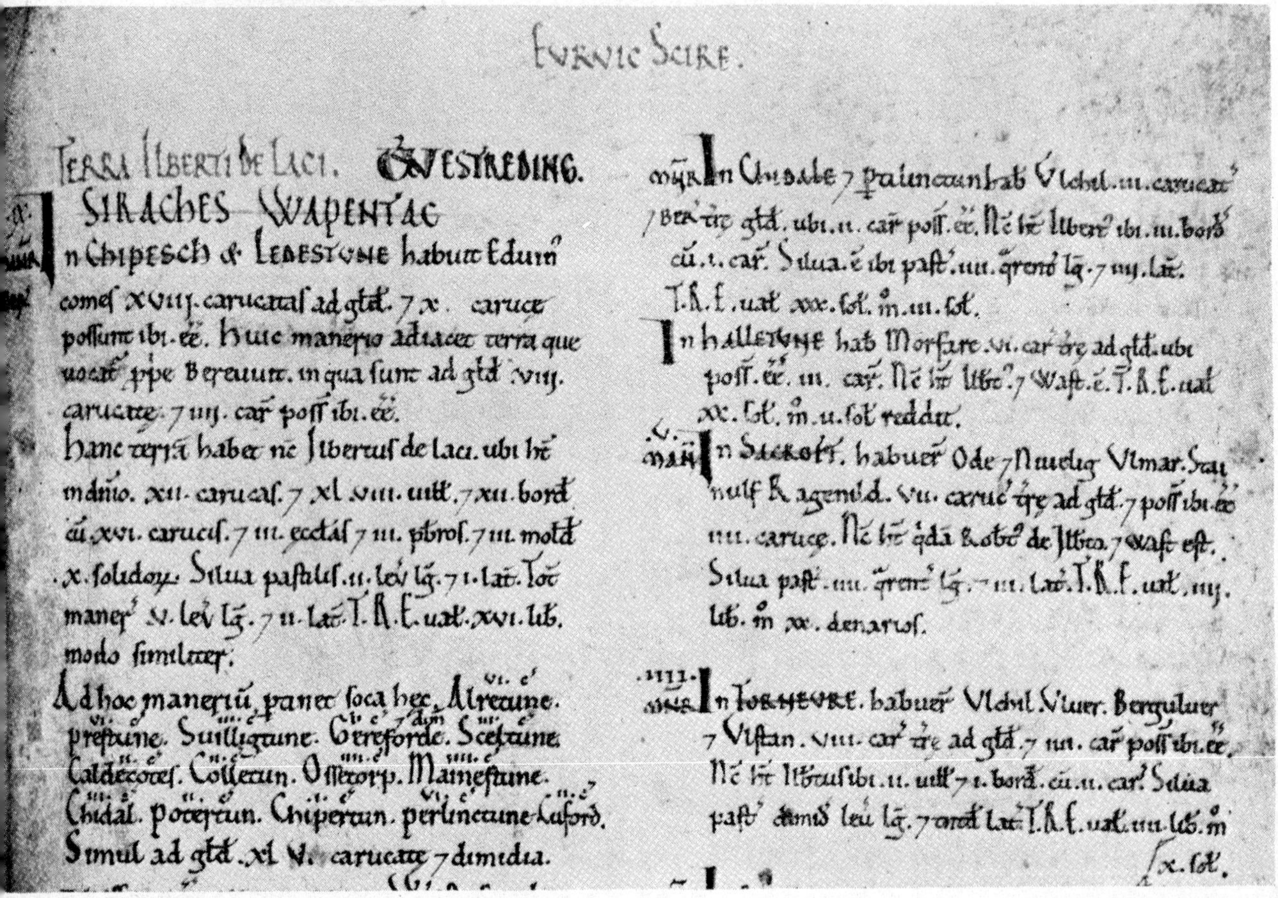

Note: Lining through a heading is used where nowadays we should underline; all the statistics are in Roman figures; the mark like a 7 means &; MAN., MANR., MNR. means MANOR(S); BER, is BEREWICK, a village or hamlet belonging to a manor.

There is a rough uniformity in the shape of the entries. First comes the name of the place, then that of its Anglo-Saxon lord, before 1066. Then comes the statement of how many ploughlands (*car*ucates) the place is taxed at (*ad geldum*). Then is recorded how many ploughlands (here perhaps about 120 acres each) there actually are: 'How many ploughs (*car*ucae,-as), there may be there?' The next entries answer the questions: Who has it now? How many *vill*eins, *bord*ars etc. has he there? How much pasture? What was it worth in King Edward's time? (*T*empore *R*egis *E*dwardi). What is it worth now?

All the entries except the first one (Kippax & Ledston) follow more or less the same pattern. All show the replacement of Anglo-Saxon lords by a Norman one, and the enormous reduction in the value of estates after the Harrying of the North (p. 20).

7. Part of a page from Domesday Book.

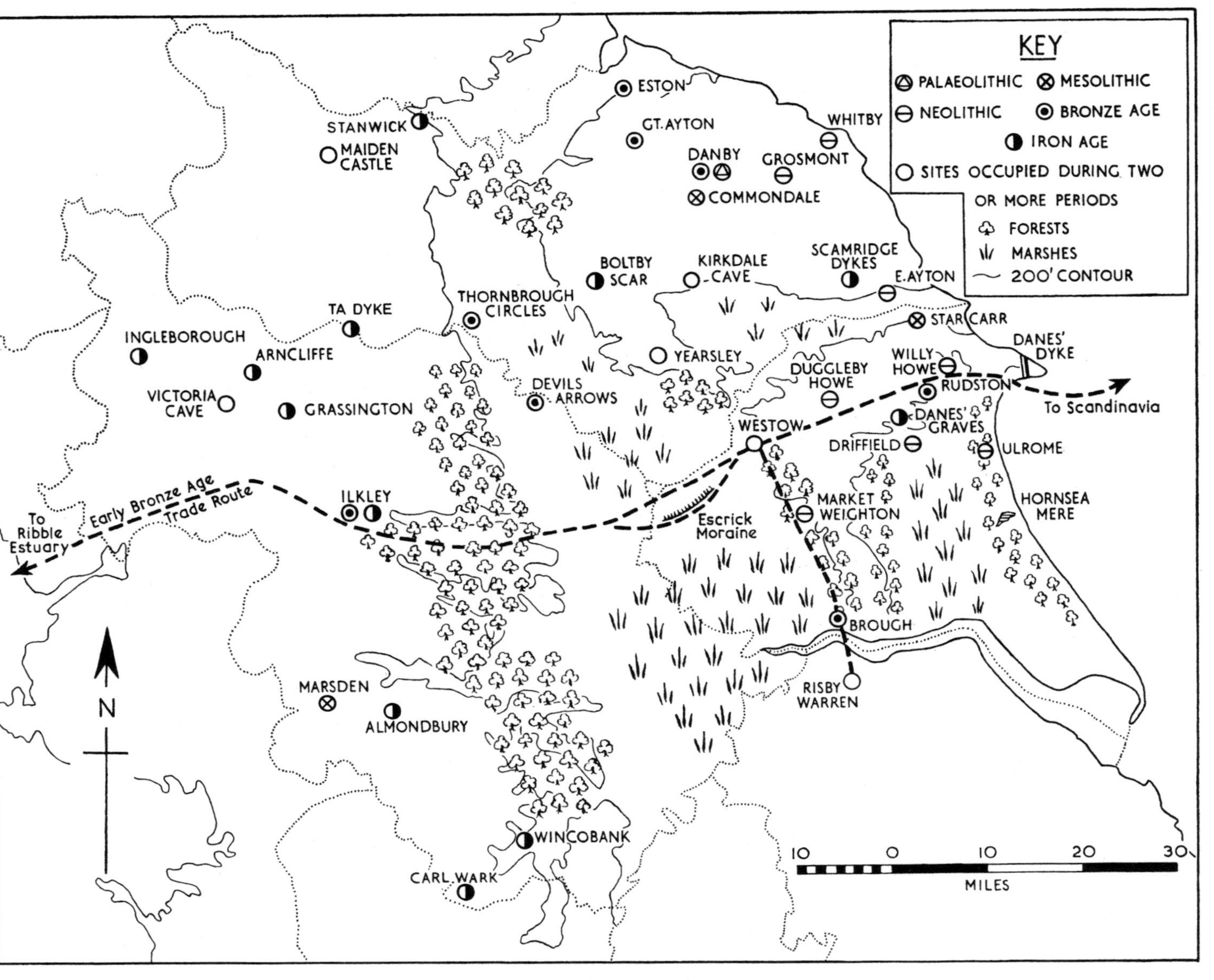

Map 2. Prehistoric Yorkshire.

Bronze Age pottery, North York Moors

The largest standing stone in Britain – a single pillar of gritstone, 25 ft. 6 ins. high – dominates the churchyard of Rudston, a Wolds village a few miles west of Bridlington. The nearest outcrop of gritstone, similar to the material of the Rudston megalith, occurs at Cayton Bay, about ten miles away. The organisation required to erect monuments of this kind, as well as the Neolithic barrows, suggests that in late Neolithic and early Bronze Age times there was in existence a highly developed society, although we know little of its structure.

The use of bronze was probably introduced into Yorkshire by some new arrivals who entered by way of the Humber estuary, about 1,800 B.C. – the Beaker Folk. They spread across the Wolds and crossed to the Pennines by routes which used the York and Escrick moraines. Their name is derived from the habit of burying beaker-shaped urns with their dead. Beaker Folk penetrated as far west as Malham Moor, but in the main they appear to have occupied sites on the Wolds, the North York Moors and the eastern slopes of the Pennines. Yorkshire museums contain many examples of 'beaker ware' pottery and of stone and bronze ornaments and implements, which these ingenious farmers left behind them. In the excavations of their farms there is evidence that they cultivated wheat. They also engaged in trade, importing flat bronze axes from Ireland; and exporting ornaments made of Whitby jet. They also traded in salt, and may have had sea connections with Scandinavia. Archaeologists are not in agreement as to whether the transition from the late Neolithic to the early Bronze Age came about as a result of invasions, or whether the new technology evolved amongst the resident population, probably stimulated by trade and peaceful contacts with other people.

About 3,000 B.C. the Beaker Folk were conquered by Celtic-speaking invaders who had entered Gaul from the Mediterranean, and who settled in Britain, to become the Brigantes (or Ancient Britons) who resisted the Roman invaders in the early years of the Christian era. The Celts knew how to make iron, and they were skilled horsemen. They went into battle mounted on iron wheeled, horse-drawn chariots, and attacked their enemies with iron swords and spears. Their farmsteads were made up of groups of small square or rectangular fields, often enclosed by low walls of gravel or stones. Their huts were made of branches, or wattle, standing on low circular foundations of stone. The roofs were thatched with straw or reeds. The outlines of such Celtic Iron Age settlements may be seen near Grassington and Malham, but perhaps the most spectacular Iron Age remains are at Stanwick, north of Richmond.

The Brigantes were not the only Celtic tribe to occupy part of Yorkshire. In Holderness and the Wolds area a tribe known as the Parisii, who had come from Belgium, were there when the first Roman soldiers crossed the Humber. These were only two of the dozen or more Celtic tribes, like the Silures of South Wales and the Iceni of East Anglia, who were conquered by the Romans during the first century A.D.

Celtic chariot found at Garton Slack

The Brigantes had a highly organised society, with a hierarchy of military rulers. The mobility which they acquired by means of their equestrian skills provided the opportunity for their rulers to exercise command over relatively large areas of northern England. The prevalence of the horse motif on brooches and ornaments of the period suggests that they recognised the importance of the horse in their society. From Roman writers we know the names of two Brigantian rulers – Cartimandua and her husband, Venutius, whom she divorced in A.D. 74. Although the Romans conquered the Brigantes and occupied their territory, the Romano-British society which developed under Roman rule involved a merging of two cultures.

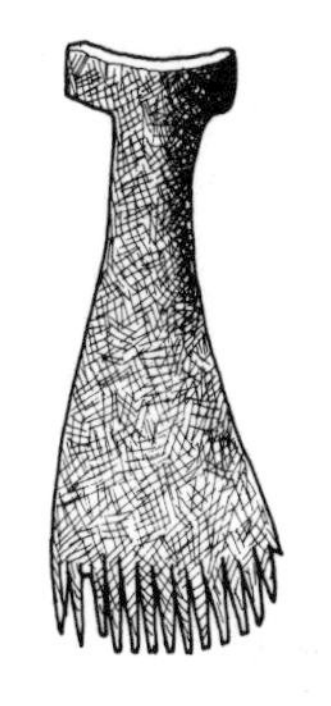

Romano-British bone comb, Settle

The Brigantes fought hard to defend themselves against the invaders, and there are several impressive fortifications which bear witness to the determined resistance which they organised. Cartimandua may have had a hand in the building of the fortifications on Castle Hill, Almondbury; and on the summit of Ingleborough. Other Brigantian fortifications are to be found at Fort Gregory, in Grass Wood, near Grassington, and at Ta Dyke, above Kettlewell. Their largest fortified settlement, however, was at Stanwick.

The use of terms such as Neolithic, Bronze Age, Iron Age, etc., is of limited validity to modern archaeologists. It should be understood that these terms are merely guides to the predominant technology which belonged to a particular culture. There was not usually a clear break with the past when new materials came into use. Often there was a merging of peoples and ways of life. Many sites were shared by two or more cultures. For example, Mesolithic flints and chert tools are found in a Bronze Age cremation urn in Sheffield, and bronze ornaments in excavations of Celtic Iron Age sites. In east Yorkshire some Iron Age sites have been associated in the popular mind with the later Danish invaders – e.g. Danes Graves near Kilham and Danes Dyke at Flamborough – but the Scandinavian connection is probably mistaken.

The last of the prehistoric occupants of Yorkshire before the arrival of the Romans were unable to read or write, but they have left their mark on the place names of Yorkshire. The main rivers of the county carry Celtic names – Aire, Calder, Don, Nidd and Wharfe (but not Swale or Ure). The British kingdom of Elmet, the capital of which was a place named Loidis (the forerunner of the modern city of Leeds), stretched from the foothills of the Pennines to the Humber Fens, covering a large part of the area later known as the West Riding. The place names Barwick-in-Elmet and Sherburn-in-Elmet are reminders of this ancient kingdom.

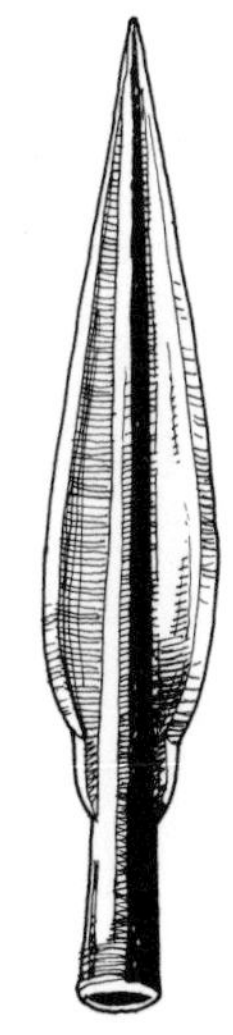

Bronze Age spear, Semerwater

III Roman Yorkshire

First-century Roman pottery, Castleshaw

In Roman times – which for Yorkshire began about A.D. 70 and ended in the early fifth century – the geography of northern England was different from that of today. Much of the Vale of York was marshy and impassable. Travel across it was only possible by using the ridges of higher ground, the moraines left by the glaciers of the last Ice Age. The Vale of Pickering was still unreclaimed from the lingering traces of the great lake which had occupied it in glacial times, and there were great stretches of swamp in the Humber Fens. In places there were thick forests, of which little today remains, except for place names on the map; for example, the Forest of Galtres, near York; the Forest of Elmet, near Leeds, and Knaresborough Forest. Even the configuration of the coastline was different (see Chapter XXI).

The Romans came to this wild and inhospitable area in order to provide a defensive bulwark with which to protect the settlements in the lowlands of eastern and southern England. They found it necessary to subdue the Celtic-speaking Brigantes in Yorkshire, and to hold at bay the warlike Picts and Scots further north. The Roman occupation of England began in earnest in A.D. 43, but it was almost thirty years later before they crossed the Humber and advanced into Yorkshire. One of the main routes along which they advanced was from *Lindum* (Lincoln), along the chalk Wolds to the Humber, to the west of the site of the present Humber Bridge. There may have been a ford – and there was certainly a ferry – across the Humber, which enabled them to cross to their landing place at *Petuaria* (Brough), where many early Roman coins and pottery fragments have been found, as well as a few traces of their settlement. From Brough the Roman route ran under the scarp of the Yorkshire Wolds, eventually crossing the Derwent valley and the Vale of York to reach the present site of York. A branch road passed through *Delgovicia* (near Millington) and over the Wolds to *Derventio* (Malton), which became an important route centre on the road between York and the coast at Scarborough and Filey, where Roman signal beacons were erected to guide coastal shipping. The main trunk road up the Vale of York, linking the settlements of *Danum* (Doncaster), *Calcaria* (Tadcaster), *Isurium Brigantium* (Aldborough) and *Cataractonium* (Catterick) is followed in part by the modern A1. For much of the way it runs along a line of low magnesian limestone, which not only afforded a dry and relatively open route, but was also a source of excellent building stone.

Roman standard bearer

The map of Roman roads (map 3) shows that in the main they followed upland areas: the chalk Wolds, the Pennines and the North York Moors. Apart from the fact that these lines of communication were easier to build on, because there was no need to clear forests or to drain marshes in order to make the roads, they were also easier to defend, as the open vistas of the hills gave warning of the approach of enemy forces.

Once they had penetrated into the Pennines, the Romans soon discovered the valuable deposits of lead ore and, within a few years of the defeat of the Brigantes at Stanwick in A.D. 74, they were smelting lead at Greenhow, above Nidderdale. Tacitus, Agricola's son-in-law, records that Brigantian prisoners taken at Stanwick were set to work mining lead and building roads to the lead mining areas. Two pigs of lead, weighing over 155 lbs. each, have been found near Greenhow and are stamped with the inscription IMP. CAES. DOMITIANO AVG, COS. VII (*Imperatore Caesare Domitiane Auguste Consule Septimum*) which indicates that they were cast in the seventh term of office as consul of the Emperor Domitian – i.e. in A.D. 81. One of these pigs can be seen in the British Museum and another in Ripley Castle. A third pig, now lost, was inscribed with the name of the Emperor Trajan, who ruled between A.D. 91 and A.D. 117. The Romans used lead for water pipes and as an alloy with tin in the manufacture of pewter ware. They are also known to have worked the iron ore deposits in the coal measures in the Bradford and Sheffield areas.

Although there were economic benefits which could be derived from the occupation of Yorkshire and the exploitation of its timber and mineral resources, the primary reason for the Roman presence was military. By A.D. 77, when the Emperor Vespasian appointed Agricola as governor of Britain, *Eboracum* (York) had become the headquarters of the famous IX Legion, and most of the Roman settlements were military stations, like *Olicana* (Ilkley), Castleshaw, Slack, *Cataractonium* (Catterick) and many temporary Roman camps, like those at Cawthorn and Goathland on the North York moors. During the second century, however, with the completion of Hadrian's Wall, the military threat lessened, and some civil settlements grew up. The largest of these was at *Isurium Brigantium* (Aldborough). There was also a large civil settlement at York (see Chapter XII), and another near Boroughbridge and there were a number of villas (country houses) in East Yorkshire. The best known of these was at Rudston, near Bridlington, and there are some outstanding Roman mosaics from villas in the Humberside area to be seen in the Hull Museum. The relations between the Romans and the Parisii, who lived in Holderness and on the Wolds, were better than those with the Brigantes and a merging of the Roman and Celtic cultures occurred. This may help to explain the greater frequency of non-military Roman settlements in East Yorkshire.

Head of Hercules from a Romano-British ring found at Malton

There is little to be seen, except their magnificent sites, of the line of signal stations which were built along the North Yorkshire coast. Typical

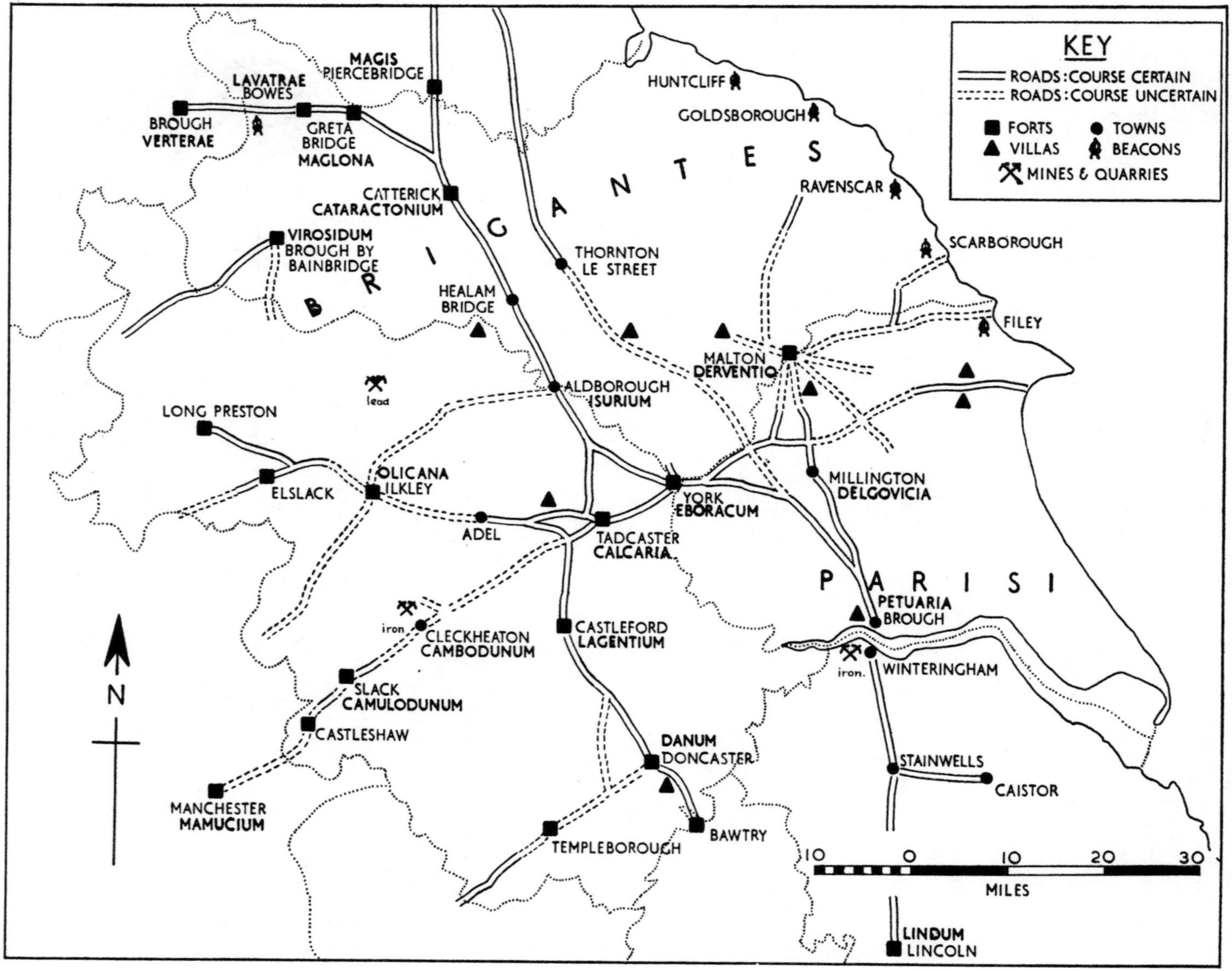

Map 3. Roman Yorkshire.

of these is the one at Goldsborough, which stands on the highest point above Lythe Bank, and guards the approach to Whitby. It commands a view over the North Sea which would give watchers there ample warning of the approach of shipping, and a beacon lit at this point could be seen for many miles out to sea. Another signal station was located on Castle Hill, Scarborough.

The Romans have not left us many place-names – Catterick, derived from *Cataractonium* is an obvious one – but their most abiding legacy in Yorkshire is the road system which the invaders left behind. Although they occasionally sited their roads along the lines of older British tracks, many of them struck out along new routes. It may be an exaggeration to say, as the Duke of Edinburgh once did, that until the motorway building of the post-war period, no new roadways had been planned in Britain since the Romans left; it is undoubtedly true that, until recently, much of our national road system followed the lines established by the Romans. Mention has already been made of the relationship between A1 and the Roman road along the Vale of York. Other modern main roads which follow the routes of Roman roads are the A166, from Stamford Bridge to Driffield; the A1079, between York and Market Weighton; the A59, between Blubberhouses and Harrogate and between Green Hammerton and York; and the A1034, between South Cave and Market Weighton. There are also some stretches of the original Roman routes which can be seen, as on the moors above Goathland, and on Blubberhouses Moor. The road across Blackstone Edge may also be a Roman road, although this is not certain. It is not always possible to tell which parts of these surviving roads have been improved and repaired during the later centuries.

In A.D. 402 the Roman garrison was recalled from York by Stillicho, the regent of Emperor Honorius, who was himself of Vandal origin, because of the desperate situation in Rome and, although some vestige of Roman influence remained for a few more years, Yorkshire passed along with much of the rest of Europe into the Dark Ages.

Roman pillar, York

IV The Anglo-Saxons in Yorkshire

Anglo-Saxon helmet found in York

Even before the last Roman legionaries were recalled from Yorkshire in the early fifth century there had been many raids by warlike Teutonic tribes from across the North Sea, from Friesland, Jutland and Saxony. In the last decades of the Empire the Romans had recruited local Britons into their legions, and when the legions were recalled some semblance of a peasant militia was left. York itself – renamed with the Celtic-sounding Caer-Ebrauc – remained for a time as a refuge for the local people, but little is known of the fate of Yorkshire during the fifth and sixth centuries. In A.D. 560 an Anglian king, Aella, established himself as ruler of Deira, a principality the name of which originally appeared to refer to Holderness, but later was applied to an area covering most of present day Yorkshire. According to the Venerable Bede, a reference to the Angles and Aella forms the basis of Gregory the Deacon's famous pun, when he saw some fair-haired, blue-eyed lads from Yorkshire in the slave market in Rome. 'Not Angles, but angels' he called them. 'Who is their King?' 'Aella' was the reply. 'Alleluia shall be sung in this country.' Christianity was brought to the Anglians of Deira not long afterwards by Romano-Celtic missionaries, of whom St Aidan from Lindisfarne was one of the pioneers. One of Aidan's pupils, St Chad, became Bishop of Mercia in A.D. 669, with his seat at Lichfield, and shortly afterwards he sent his brother, St Cedd, to become Abbot of Lastingham, near Pickering. In the early seventh century the kingdom of Northumbria, to which Deira had been joined, was ruled by Edwin, son of Aella.

Edwin was himself a heathen, but he married Ethelburga, the daughter of Ethelbert and Bertha, the Christian rulers of Kent. Edwin agreed to allow Paulinus, a Christian priest, to live in his court, and the combined efforts of the young queen and her priest eventually ensured the conversion of Edwin. It was not an easy task, however, for although Edwin was tolerant and well disposed to the new faith, he had to consider the views of his council of elders – the Witan – and of the adherents of his old heathen faith. When he married, the Pope sent gifts and a letter advising him to listen to the teaching of Paulinus, but he still hesitated. He regarded his escape from assassination, which came as he received news of the birth of his first daughter, as a good omen, and consented to the baby's christening. He promised Paulinus that if he won a victory over the West Saxons and became virtual ruler of all England outside

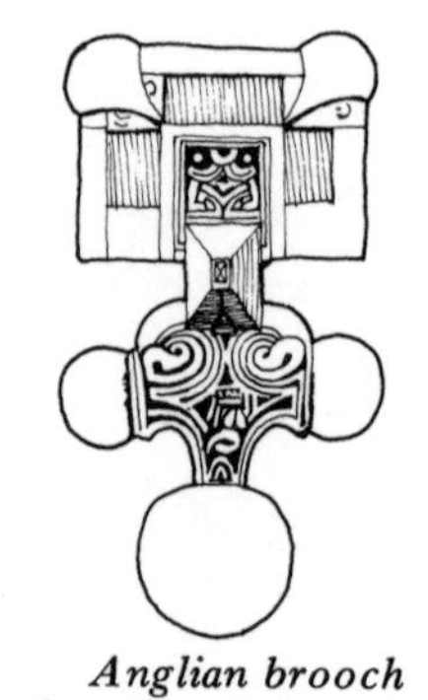

Anglian brooch found at Catterick

Kent, he would become a Christian. In A.D. 627, having temporarily achieved his ambition, Edwin called together his Witan and persuaded many of them to be baptised with him, including the high priest of the old faith, Coifi. Coifi declared that no-one could have served the old gods more faithfully than he had done, but they seemed to have done very little for him. So Coifi at once threw off the old faith, and rode off to the heathen temple at Goodmanham, near Market Weighton. In the presence of an amazed crowd, he cast his lance into the sacred wooden building, and called on the bystanders to join him in destroying it; which they did with great enthusiasm. Christianity had come to be the faith of Yorkshiremen, and on Easter Day 627 Edwin himself was baptised in a little wooden church which had been hastily put up in his capital city of York – the first York Minster.

Christianity, however, had not won Yorkshire permanently, nor was the form of Christianity – Celtic or Roman – finally decided by Edwin's conversion. Another challenge came from the influential British leader, Cadwalla, who ruled in North Wales, but who had influence far beyond that area. He formed an alliance with Penda of Mercia, and together they challenged Edwin's supremacy in Northumbria. In A.D. 632, at Hatfield Chase (Haethfeldland), between Thorne and Doncaster, Edwin was defeated and slain, his army annihilated and his capital, Eoforwic (York), occupied by Cadwalla. A dispute over the succession to the Northumbrian throne followed. The northern half of the kingdom, Bernicia, which stretched from the Tyne to Edinburgh (Edwin's town), was seized by Eanfrith, who travelled to York in A.D. 634 to attempt to strike a bargain with Cadwalla, who promptly had his visitor beheaded. This left Oswald, a member of the Bernician ruling family, as the only pretender to the throne of Northumbria with a credible claim, but in order to secure his position Oswald had to get rid of Cadwalla. This he succeded in doing at the battle of Hexham in A.D. 634.

On the news of the death of Edwin, Paulinus travelled to Rochester in Kent, with Edwin's queen, leaving behind in Yorkshire his friend, James the Deacon, to carry on his missionary work. A century later Bede records the courage of James in keeping Christianity alive at a time of great crisis, when the faith had only just established itself in Yorkshire. The Venerable Bede may, however, have got his facts wrong when he attributes the place name Akebar, near Leyburn, as being derived from *Jakobi burgus* (James' mound) and marking the place where James preached. The probable derivation is Oak Hill. Nevertheless, Bede's account of James' work is true in essentials.

Effigy of St Oswald from the village church at Bolton Percy

Christianity became the official religion of Northumbria under Oswald, who reigned until A.D. 641, and who was canonised as St Oswald in recognition of his services to the faith. His services to York, however, are open to some question, as he removed his capital to Bamburgh Castle in Bernicia. York became a local capital of the province of Deira, but the division of Northumbria into two provinces, and the rivalries

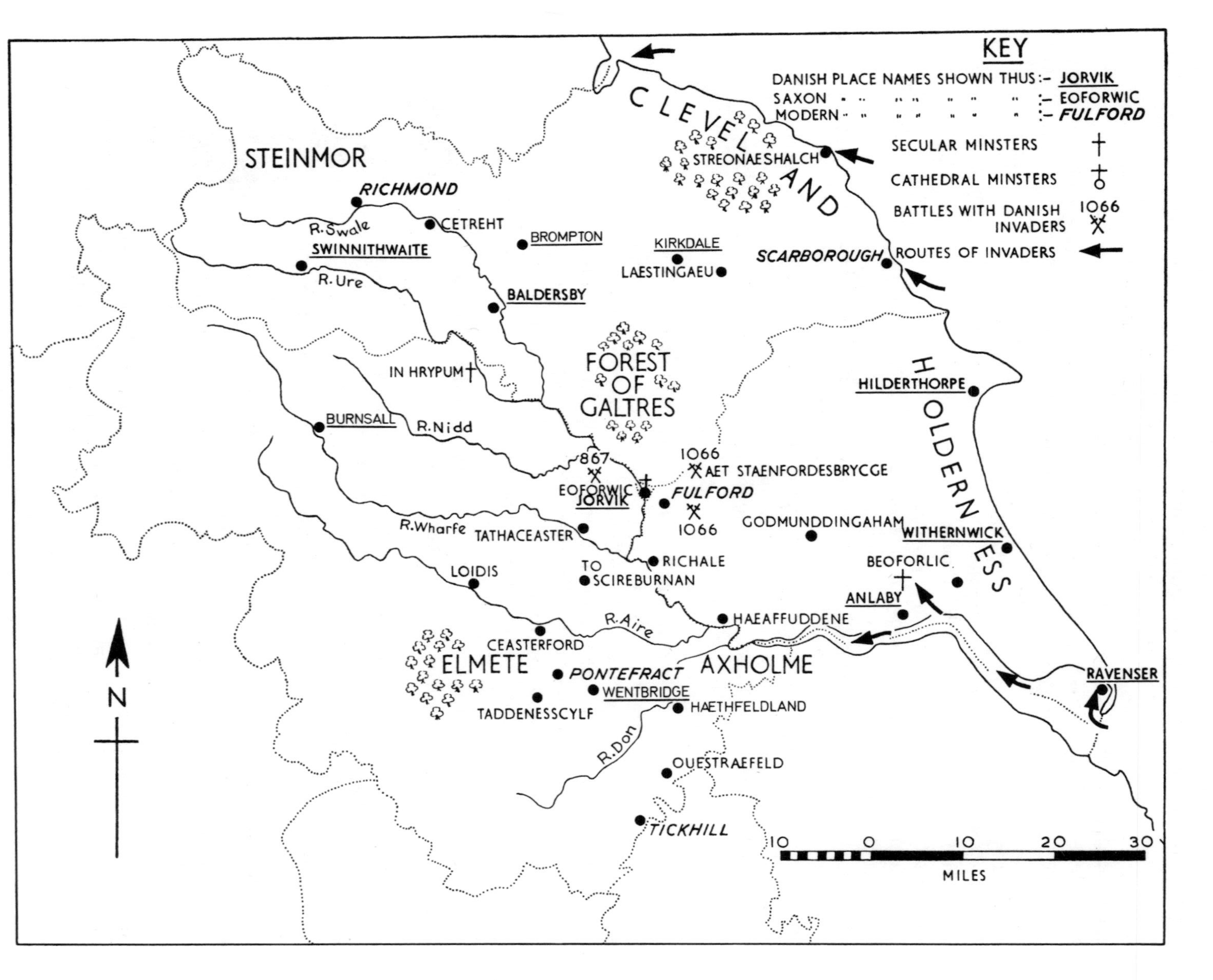

Map 4. Anglo-Saxon and Viking Yorkshire.

between Bamburgh and York contributed to the weakening of the kingdom. In A.D. 651 the sub-ruler of Deira, the devious Oidiwald, formed an alliance with the aged Penda of Mercia in an attempt to overthrow Oswald's successor and to win the throne of Northumbria from Oswald's brother, Oswy. The armies met at Wentbridge and Oswy decisively defeated the rebels. The struggle between Bernicia and Deira continued, however, during the eighth century and was still a source of weakness when the Danes invaded in the next century.

Although Deira was politically disrupted by these disputes they seemed not to have affected the life of the Church. Yorkshire during the Anglo-Saxon period became a centre of scholarship and education, fostered by the Church. This was particularly true of York itself, but also of abbeys elsewhere. In A.D. 732 York became recognised as the ecclesiastical centre of the Northern Province of the Church.

The impetus for this religious activity came originally from Oswald. He had called in missionaries to help him to convert his kingdom to Christianity. These he obtained from the monks of Lindisfarne and Iona, where influences from Celtic Christianity were strong. There were many differences of custom and government between the Christians of the north of England and those of the south, who owed allegiance to the Pope in Rome. Yorkshire, where the two sets of missionaries clashed, was also the place where their disputes were settled: at the Synod (Church meeting) of Whitby, A.D. 663. Here the Roman party won the day. The story goes that the Roman representatives claimed to represent St Peter (said to be the first Bishop of Rome), who had the keys of Heaven (hence St Peter's keys), while no-one ventured to make any such claim on behalf of the northern Bishop, St Columba. King Oswy decided in favour of Rome, in the hope that when his turn came St Peter would show favour to him. So the king himself said, but certainly the remark was a joking one. The real point of the decision is that by it the English Church agreed to give up minor points which might separate it from the rest of the Christian world; and, like the rest of Western Christianity, to accept the Pope as its head. He retained this position in relation to the Church of England for nearly nine hundred years, until King Henry VIII's Act of Supremacy in 1534 put an end to it.

For 200 years the story of the Christian faith in England centres very largely in Yorkshire. Churches and monasteries were built, parts of which still remain, for example, at Lastingham and Whitby. With Christianity came learning; and then missionary work. The English, lately heathens, set about the conversion of the heathens in Germany, Holland and Denmark. Many of the earliest Christian missionaries to the continent were Northumbrians. The influence of the great scholar Bede of Jarrow (673-735) reached York, where later another great scholar, Alcuin, A.D. 735-804, made a centre of learning unrivalled anywhere in Northern Europe, and second only to Rome itself. As he said, York was *Altera Roma* – the other Rome. However, the glory of York and Yorkshire in relation to religion and learning was short-lived.

'Old Ralph' Cross above Glaisdale, North Yorkshire

V Viking Yorkshire

A Viking ship

In the ninth century the growth of all the Christian kingdoms of the English was disrupted by invaders from Scandinavia. Most of those who came to Yorkshire crossed the North Sea from Denmark, but others came from Norway, sailed round the Scottish coast and landed in Ireland, the Isle of Man and the west coasts of Scotland and England, some settling in the Yorkshire Pennines. Place-name evidence can sometimes identify the areas where the Scandinavians settled. For example, the endings -sett and -side in Burtersett and Gunnerside (Gunnar's Saetr) are from the Norwegian '*saetr*', an alpine pasture; whilst many names in the East Riding with the ending '-by' are from the Danish language. Both groups of Scandinavian invaders are known as Vikings, 'Vik' meaning a creek or inlet from which the invaders set sail in their long boats.

The incursions of the Vikings had been taking place for many decades before the mid-ninth century, but usually the invaders were content to raid, loot and pillage coastal settlements, monasteries and farms, before setting off back to Scandinavia to avoid the onset of winter. The first description of a Viking raid dates from A.D. 793. By the middle of the ninth century expeditions of 300 ships were bringing armies to our shores. In A.D. 865, however, a Danish army wintered in East Anglia for the first time. From there Ivar the Boneless led an army against Deira. It is thought that another Danish army also came by sea into the mouth of the Humber and sailed up the river to York. York fell to the invaders in A.D. 866, and soon became the chief city of the area known as the Danelaw.

The Vikings were pagans when they first came to Yorkshire but they soon adopted the Christian faith of the Anglo-Saxons they had conquered. They also took over and developed the art of stone carving, and some of the most enduring memorials to the Viking Age in Yorkshire are to be found in the carved stone crosses with their characteristic ring heads (a circle of stone linking the arms of the cross); and the decorated hog-back tombs. The hog-backs at Brompton church, near Northallerton, are notable for the carvings of muzzled bears, which adorn the gable ends. The Viking art of Yorkshire shows a merging of styles, but there are characteristic Scandinavian motifs which can be identified.

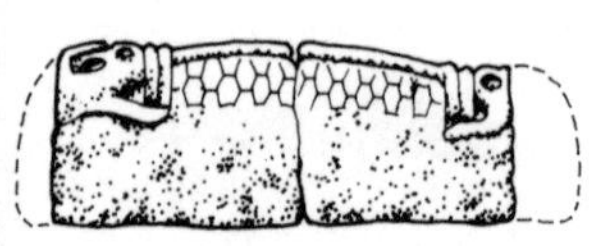

Viking hog-back tomb, Burnsall

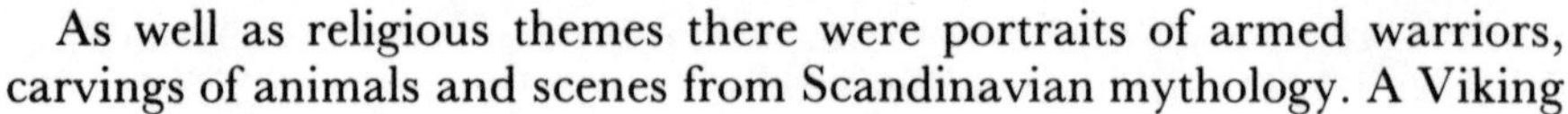

As well as religious themes there were portraits of armed warriors, carvings of animals and scenes from Scandinavian mythology. A Viking cross discovered in Leeds depicts the legendary Wayland Smith surrounded by winged angels. The ring chain ornamentation which is found at Burnsall, and some of the animal designs on ornaments found in York are in the so-called Borre style of decoration, after a place in southern Norway, where a rich find of grave goods was discovered. A fragment of a cross found at Weston church in Wharfedale, during church restoration a century ago, and now kept in Weston Hall, suggests that the Viking sculptor had re-used an Anglian cross, preserving some of the original decorative carving, but adding figures of an armed warrior and a woman in Scandinavian style.

The boundaries of Yorkshire, which were settled during the Viking period and which remained until 1974, are roughly those of the Danish kingdom of York (Jorvik) which was ruled over by more than a dozen kings between A.D. 875, when Halfdan, the son of the legendary Ragnar Lothbrok, who founded the kingdom, ruled, and A.D. 954 when the kingdom was lost by Eric Bloodaxe. For the rest of the period until the Norman Conquest Yorkshire was re-absorbed into the English kingdom and the Danelaw ceased to exist.

However, as recent discoveries in York have abundantly shown, the life of the Anglo-Danish culture of Viking Age Yorkshire continued with vigour. A lively trade developed across the Irish Sea and crossed the North Sea, as the discovery of coins minted in York bears witness. The agricultural activity of the Anglo-Danish villages is shown by the discoveries at Wharram Percy, on the Wolds; and at Ribblehead in the Pennines. The use of words of Scandinavian origin in the dialect of Yorkshire (e.g. lathe, stack) suggests that the new arrivals settled down to farm alongside the Anglians – probably in reasonable amity once the first shock of the invasion and conquest was over.

Even in Yorkshire the number of Danes who settled was quite small in proportion to the English population which still remained. Moreover, in speech and customs and even in physical appearance the Danes were not very different from the English themselves. So, after the fighting was over and the Danes had established their mastery, they seem to have settled down quite happily side by side with the English. They intermarried, they accepted Christianity and long before 1066, largely perhaps because of the wisdom of King Edgar (A.D. 959-979) who treated the English and Danes as being equal before the law, they had come to regard themselves as Englishmen. The mixture of Danish and English place-names in Yorkshire suggests that often a Danish settlement was established without any fighting, on the waste ground between two English villages. The Danes were absorbed into the English nation, quite unlike the Britons who had been slaughtered or driven out, or at best enslaved.

Viking cross, Middleton

There are still some Yorkshire survivals from the days of the Danish settlement, and from the rule of the Danish Kings. Probably the three Ridings were established then. Each Riding was represented in the

Thing – a kind of parliament, held at York. Within each there were (and are) smaller divisions – the wapentakes. These largely replaced the old Anglo-Saxon divisions, the hundreds. Yorkshire is one of the seven English counties, all largely of Danish settlement, in which we hear little of hundreds, but a great deal of wapentakes. Each wapentake had its own meeting of freemen to arrange for defence and to administer justice. Often the name of the wapentake still preserves a reference to the place where this assembly met. Thus the North Riding Wapentake of Hallikeld met at a holy spring. Skyrack (Shire Oak) Wapentake in the West Riding was so called from the oak where the freemen assembled. At the *Original Oak* Inn in Leeds a plaque, made from the wood of an ancient tree, records the fact that the inn stands exactly on the place of assembly of the Danish freemen of this part of Yorkshire, about 1,000 years ago.

In its later days the Kingdom of York became more and more dependent on the rest of England. The last of the English kings to reign before the arrival of the Normans in 1066 was Harold, son of Godwin, who was partly Danish. He lost his throne and his life after a reign of only 40 weeks, largely because he punished his brother, Tostig, for ill-treating the northern subjects into whose care Harold had placed them. Tostig's offences included the murder of a local chieftain in Yorkshire, Gamel, in 1065. The names of Tostig and Gamel appear on an inscription on the sundial, which dates from 1055, which refers to the rebuilding of St Gregory's Minster by 'Orm the son of Gamel . . . in the days of King Edward and Earl Tostig'. Tostig formed an alliance with the Norwegian king, Harold Hardrada, and together they invaded Yorkshire in 1066. Having harried the coast from Cleveland to Spurn, they sailed up the Humber and the Ouse to Riccall, and from there marched on York. After defeating an English army under Edwin and Morcar at Fulford, they camped at Stamford Bridge and there awaited King Harold, on 25 September 1066.

There is a story told of how, when the battle went against Tostig and his allies, a brave Dane held the bridge alone in order to cover his friends' retreat – until he was stabbed from below by an Englishman who had ventured out in a boat on the river. The battle was a crushing defeat for Tostig, who was slain, and for Harold Hardrada, who received, as the English king had promised him, his grant of land in England – seven feet – enough for a grave, or, 'since he was a tall man, perhaps a little more'. It was a great success for the English Harold, who marched off to York with his army in triumph, to celebrate his great victory. However, the celebration in York was soon followed by disaster. In less than three weeks Harold lay dead on the field of Hastings. Around him in a circle lay the corpses of the comrades of his bodyguard who had revelled with him in York.

Although Harold was the last Anglo-Danish king of England, the Anglo-Danish strain in the ancestry of the people of Yorkshire remained, and indeed remains to this day. Traces of Danish speech are still to be found, especially in the dialect of the folk who live by the Yorkshire coast. The Yorkshire open 'a' is Danish; so is the Yorkshire name for a brook, *beck*; and the Yorkshire use of gate for street. Many Yorkshire village names are of Danish origin, the -thwaites; the -bys; and most of the -wicks, -kirks, and -thorpes. On the other hand, the -leys, and the -tons and the -hams are of Anglo-Saxon origin.

The Vikings on the whole avoided the Roman towns and fortresses which they found when they invaded, with the notable exception of York. Most of the others were in decay in any case, and were allowed to continue in this condition. They used parts of the Roman roads, but also developed their own system of trackways, to suit their different needs as traders and farmers. Roman roads were often used as boundary markers between parishes, and some straight line parish boundaries on today's map are derived from these origins.

The tracks made by the Anglo-Saxons themselves – like those of the Britons before them – often tended to be of a cross or a star shape, radiating from a valley settlement, as the British ones had done from a hilltop village. Often one arm of the cross ran down to the river and the rich natural meadow, another went up the hillside through the common pasture to the unreclaimed woodland. The other two led more or less horizontally along the valley, through the open arable fields and the remaining wasteland, to link up with similar tracks stretching outwards from the next two neighbouring villages, up and down the valley. This explains why, to this day, many of the by-roads in Yorkshire zigzag through the countryside in a series of more or less right-angle bends. Many of these roads are following the tracks made by our ancestors through their acre strips. These made up the unfenced, open arable fields, gradually set out as the land was first taken into cultivation.

The strips themselves have, of course, disappeared long ago, many of them during the 18th century in the Agricultural Revolution and the enclosure movement which accompanied it. Often, however, the plan of the strips is to be seen in the ridge-and-furrow of fields now in grass, which long ago were under the plough.

In Yorkshire our typical 'rolling English road' sets out first along the boundary between two neighbouring strips, and follows this for a furlong or so until it reaches the headland (the end of the strip, where the plough oxen turned). It turns here at right angles, and follows the headland, perhaps for the breadth of only one strip, perhaps for that of a dozen or more. Then it turns again, and resumes, more or less, its original direction, along the boundary between another couple of strips.

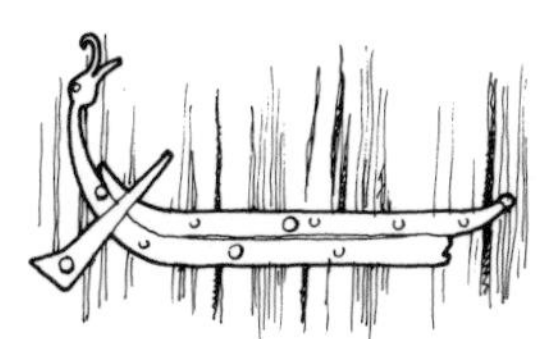

Viking ship from the church door at Stillingfleet

Thus it can be seen that in Yorkshire our local government divisions, our speech, our place-names and even the very shape of our fields and roads, are often an inheritance from our Anglo-Saxon ancestors and their Danish cousins.

VI The Normans in Yorkshire

While Harold and his men were in York, feasting and carousing in celebration of their victory over the Danes at Stamford Bridge, news came of the landing in Sussex of another invader, Duke William of Normandy. Harold hurried south to meet his new enemy, and at Hastings in October 1066 he was killed in battle, and his army defeated. On Christmas Day William had himself crowned King of England, but, in Yorkshire and the north, rebels (often aided by Danish invaders) defied the Normans, and William was forced to make many warlike expeditions in order to suppress his opponents.

The Archbishop of York, Aldred, had crowned William in Westminster Abbey, and some of the great Yorkshire earls paid homage to him, but many other Englishmen did not accept the Norman rule. In 1068 Edwin and Morcar, two of the earls who had sworn allegiance to William, rose against him; so William marched north, eventually reaching York. Here he built fortifications and left a garrison under the sheriff, William Malet. No sooner had the King left than another rebellion broke out, and William had to come back to York again. This time he sacked the town and killed hundreds of the inhabitants, before erecting another fort (almost certainly the mound on which Clifford's Tower now stands) and leaving the town in the hands of a garrison of his soldiers.

In 1069 yet another rebellion occurred, this time supported by the Danes, who sailed up the Humber and along the Ouse to York. York was captured and 3,000 Normans slain. William soon avenged this insult. He came into Lincolnshire, and finding the Danes commanding the Humber, turned west, then north, crossing the Aire near Pontefract, and advanced through the forest and marshes of the Vale of York to take the city. He found York deserted; the Danes had fled. Afterwards a chronicler described the terrible scene of devastation which William left behind – bodies rotting by the roadside, as no one was left to bury them, men forced to eat horses, dogs and cats. Between York and Durham every town stood empty, with wild beasts running in the streets. In 1086, when the Domesday Survey was being made, the effect of the 'Harrying of the North' could be seen in the constant references to 'waste' after the names of the towns and villages of Yorkshire. For generations a great part of Yorkshire was looked upon by the Norman barons as a place for hunting only. Most of the land was not cultivated and it was many years before its people recovered from the terrible punishment William had inflicted upon them.

The Norman barons usually built themselves castles; partly as a defence against invaders, such as the Scots, partly to protect themselves against their tenants, or other barons, even perhaps against the King. These castles were not all massive stone buildings. Often they were made of wood, with a moat and earthworks as the main defences. The castle which William built at York in 1069 must certainly have been of wood, because it took only eight days to complete. The usual plan of a Norman castle is a tower or keep, standing on a mound round which there is a ditch, and there is often a wall or stockade between the mound and the ditch or moat. Later the outer walls were strengthened, and in some castles they came to be more important than the keep. There are substantial remains of the work of Norman barons to be seen today in such castles at Richmond, Scarborough and Conisborough.

Norman keep at Conisborough Castle

The lands of Yorkshire, as set out in Domesday Book, are recorded as having been held by the King himself, and by 29 other principal 'tenants-in-chief' under him. Among the laymen, the most important of these were the Count of Mortain, Ilbert de Lacy and Roger de Busli.

Robert, Count of Mortain, half-brother of King William, had about 215 manors in Yorkshire, scattered very widely throughout the county. He had, it is said, contributed 120 ships to William's fleet, and had commanded part of the cavalry at the Battle of Hastings. He had served William well, and his grants in England were larger than those of any other of William's followers. Count Alan the Red, of Brittany, was another of William's soldiers and a friend of the Queen; it was perhaps at her suggestion that William granted him many of the forfeited estates of Earl Edwin (page 32). Many of his manors lay together in the North Riding, around what is now the town of Richmond. Soon after he had gained his lands, Count Alan built his castle at Richmond to help him to govern his possessions and to protect the north of the county against any invading Scots. Together with King William I and King William II, Alan founded St Mary's Abbey at York (Chapter IX). Ilbert de Lacy seems to have been a friend and follower of Odo, Bishop of Bayeux, another half-brother of King William. Ilbert's lands were mainly in the West Riding. He built his castle at Tateshalle, now known as Pontefract (though Domesday Book does not mention this fact), and he also founded the Cluniac monastery there in 1100 (Chapter IX). Roger de Busli was another great Norman noble. His estates lay mostly in Nottinghamshire, where he had 163 manors, but he had another 54 in South Yorkshire. He founded the Benedictine Priory of Blyth, Nottinghamshire, in 1088 and his castle is described as being at Blyth, but was in fact probably at Laughton-en-le-Morthen. Later he removed to the castle still remaining at Tickhill, three or four miles from Blyth.

Domesday Book gives a picture of the type of land holding which formed the basis of the feudal system. There were elements of feudalism

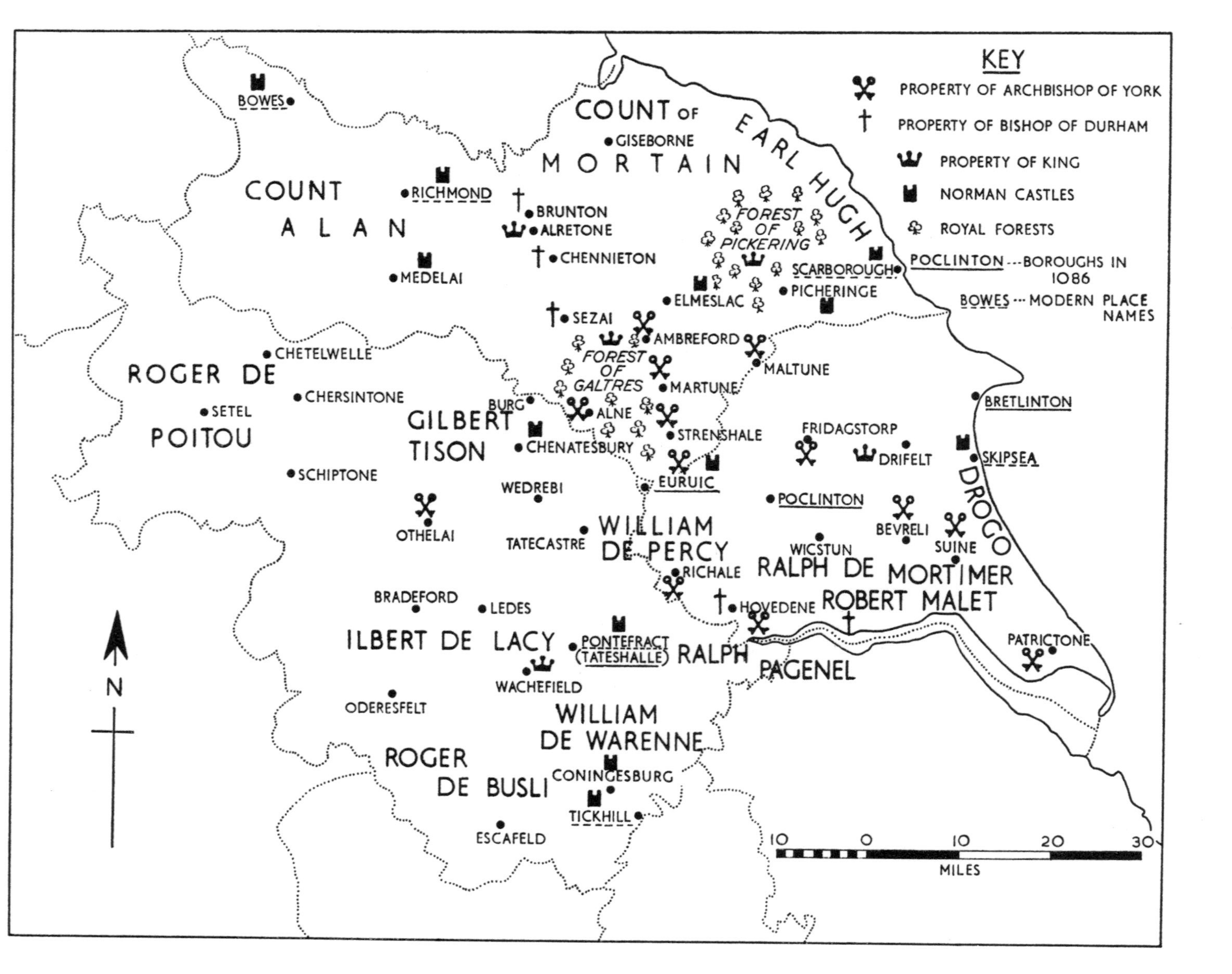

Map 5. The Normans in Yorkshire.

which existed in Anglo-Saxon England, but the Normans, because they were able to make a radical break with the past, were able to organise a system of tenure which was more rationally arranged than in other parts of Europe, or in England before the Norman Conquest. The extract from Domesday Book (plate 7) refers to the lands of Ilbert de Laci in the Leeds area. The lands would be divided into arable strips, as this system of farming had been introduced into Yorkshire before the Conquest. The hierarchy of lords, villeins, bordars, etc. was based on the concept that the King held the land in trust from God, the lords of the manor and other tenants-in-chief repaying the King for the right to hold land (the word 'tenant' is derived from the Latin *tenere*, French *tenir*, to hold) by rendering military service. The subordinates in the manorial hierarchy were bound by rights and obligations, based also on their relationship to the holding of land from the manorial lords. There were also some special rights enjoyed by monks and by citizens of the so-called Domesday boroughs, of which there were five in Yorkshire in 1086 – Scarborough, York (Eurvic), Pocklington, Pontefract (Tateshalle) and Bridlington (Bretlinton). Many of the lords were granted the right to build castles, often as a reward for services rendered during the Conquest. Some, as we shall see, abused the right and became strong enough to defy the King. As far as the ordinary people of Yorkshire were concerned, they often found their new Norman French overlords overbearing and oppressive, and they did not easily assimilate the alien manners of their masters. After the savage punishment meted out to them during the Harrying of the North, those who survived were too cowed to attempt any resistance.

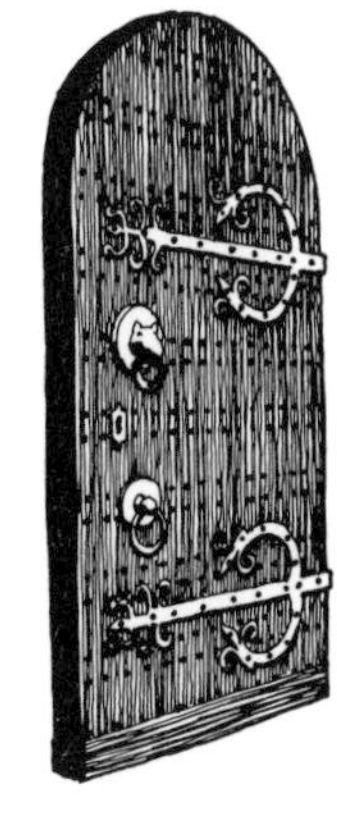

Door of the Norman church at Adel

VII Yorkshire in the Middle Ages

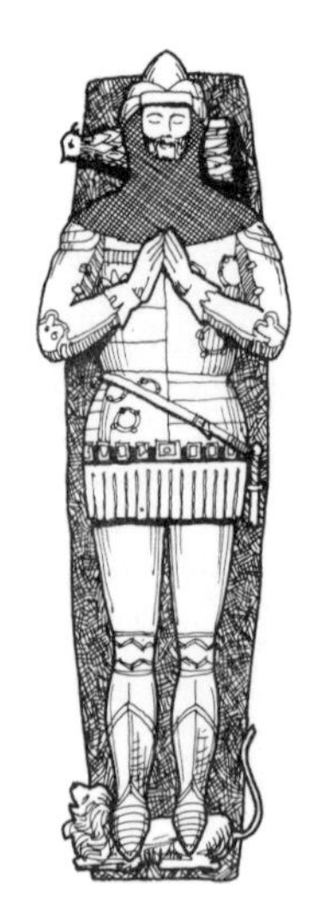

Effigy of a medieval knight

As Yorkshire began to recover from the devastation inflicted by the Harrying of the North, the process of incorporating the county into the social, administrative and ecclesiastical life of Norman England began. Large tracts of land were given by William to his supporters, many of whom were Frenchmen who had come over in the invading army in 1066, like Ilbert de Lacy. The main stronghold of the de Lacys was at Pontefract, and they also built fortresses at Almondbury and Barwick in Elmet. Upper Airedale was controlled from Skipton, by the Romilles; and the domain of the Warennes occupied the south-eastern corner along the Derbyshire and Lincolnshire borders, from Tickhill and Conisborough to Thorne Moors and the Hatfield Chase. The Percys held most of the Ouse valley south of York and also had estates in the East Riding around Beverley. The use of the name Percy as an element in many place names on the modern map of Yorkshire gives some indication of their influence (e.g. Wharram Percy, Bolton Percy).

The Norman barons were given their feudal privileges in return for imposing the King's Peace on their subordinates and in defending the realm against foreign enemies – and in Yorkshire this meant in particular the marauding Scots. If the Scottish invaders were able to breach the defences of the County Palatine of Durham, where the Prince Bishop held sway, the way was open through the Vales of Mowbray and York, into the heart of England. William I built his New Castle on the Tyne as a bastion against the Scots, and he and his successors encouraged the Yorkshire barons to erect fortifications at strategic locations throughout the county. At first they were fortresses of the motte and bailey type, with wooden palisades on the tops of natural or artificial mounds, surrounded by a moat. Early motte and bailey castles are known at Pontefract, Richmond, Skipsea and Tickhill, as well as the original Clifford's Tower at York. During the 12th century, most of the wooden castles were replaced by stone structures, and it is the ruins of these castles which are to be seen today. Richmond Castle, in its imposing setting on a loop of the Swale, was probably built of stone from the beginning. Oddly enough it is one of the few castles that never suffered a serious siege, and it remains today in a better state of preservation than do most other Norman castles.

The barons, who were given virtually the powers of princes in their new estates, were not always prepared to do what the King required of them. There were frequent revolts as the barons struggled with the King for supremacy, and many of the original families were dispossessed of their estates and replaced by others, who were considered to be more trustworthy. During the reign of William Rufus (1087-1100), the Conqueror's second son, Robert de Mowbray was thrown into prison, where he died, after attempting a rebellion. His widow later re-married and her new husband was granted lands in north Yorkshire and in the Isle of Axholme, some of which had been taken from the Stutevilles, who had lost their land when they unsuccessfully supported the claims of the Conqueror's eldest son, Robert, against those of William Rufus. Occasionally disaffected nobles joined forces with the Scots and suffered the loss of their estates, as happened to Eustace FitzJohn of Knaresborough Castle in 1136.

Although it was officially necessary to receive royal permission before building a castle, many of the barons acted on their own initiative and built 'adulterine' castles. If the King felt strong enough he would either order the demolition of castles built without his approval, or would turn out the owners and take possession for the crown. William le Gros, who built a castle at Scarborough, was forced to surrender it in 1155 and it was later replaced by a royal castle. In 1154 Philip de Tolleville's castle at Drax was taken by storm and destroyed, and the Mowbrays saw their castles at Kirkby Malzeard and Thirsk demolished in the 1170s. These were amongst the first acts of Henry II which made their impact on Yorkshire after the disastrous reign of Stephen of Blois, who occupied the throne between 1135 and 1154.

Stephen's reign was known as the Nineteen Long Winters. During this period the Scots, under King David I, twice invaded England. On the first occasion, in 1136, the Scots were bought off, but they left behind a garrison at Malton, where Eustace FitzJohn was left in charge. The most serious incursion was in 1138, when the Scots, aided by some English traitors, advanced through Northumberland and Durham and arrived in the North Riding. King Stephen was otherwise occupied, and the Yorkshire barons were left to their own devices. They gathered in York, where the redoubtable Archbishop Thurston took the lead. He ordered his priests to muster the men of each parish and to lead them against the invaders. Thurston himself, although old and infirm, was with difficulty dissuaded from acting as a general. The army which marched to meet the Scots near Northallerton included many of the famous Yorkshire barons – the Mowbrays, the de Lacys and the Percys. Battle was joined in a field three miles north of Northallerton, on 22 August 1138, and after two hours of fierce fighting the Scots were routed. Thurston's suffragan, the Bishop of Orkney, said Mass for the Norman and English soldiers in front of a ship's mast fastened to a 'mighty huge chariot supported with wheels'. On top of the mast was a pyx – a silver box, containing the wafer bread of the Mass, 'that Christ Himself might be their leader in the fight'. On crosspieces below the pyx were fixed the

Arms of the Metcalfes

Market cross and stocks, Ripley

sacred banners of St Peter of York, St Cuthbert of Durham, St Wilfred of Ripon and St John of Beverley. The battle thus became known as the Battle of the Standard.

The victory at Northallerton removed the Scottish threat for a time, although in 1175 William the Lion advanced from Scotland with a powerful force, hoping to take advantage of Henry II's involvement in wars in France and rebellion at home. William was stopped at Alnwick. He was imprisoned in Richmond Castle and later brought to York, where he was forced to pay homage to Henry before the altar of York Minster. As a token of his submission his helmet, spear and saddle were left on the altar.

Yorkshire barons showed a degree of independence during the 13th century, in the reigns of the evil John and the weak Henry III. They were involved in several revolts, at times allying themselves with the Scots. In 1213, when John attempted to recover Poitou, which had been lost in 1206, seven of the chief Yorkshire barons, including de Lacy, Percy and Mowbray, refused to follow him, and some of them were amongst the 'Guardians of the Charter' who unsuccessfully petitioned Louis of France to seize the throne of England. John was often in Yorkshire, trying to enforce his rule over the unruly barons. On the last occasion, in 1216, he seized several Yorkshire castles, including Skelton, Danby and Pontefract, but was unable to take Helmsley.

York, the second city in England, had become an important commercial and administrative centre during the 12th century, as well as a garrison town and the ecclesiastical capital of northern England. Amongst its citizens were hundreds of Jews who were allowed to live in the city under the protection of the King. Although they prospered as money lenders, because 'usury' was forbidden to Christians; and, as merchants, they were often viewed with primitive fear and hatred by their Christian neighbours. The events which led to the slaughter of Jews in York in 1190 began in London, where it was put about that the presence of Jews at the celebrations for Richard I's coronation would be a bad omen for the new reign. In fact, some Jews appeared, including two from York, bearing gifts, and were set upon by a mob. One died at Northampton on the way home. In March 1190 a mob attacked and killed his widow and children. The other Jews – some reports say 500 men and their families – took refuge in Clifford's Tower, where they were besieged by a large body of people from York and the surrounding district, incited by their priests. Threatened with death, many of the Jews killed themselves, fathers often slaughtering their wives and families before killing themselves. When the crowd finally broke in to the Tower the surviving Jews were murdered and the Jewish quarter of the town was burned down. The King, who was then taking part in the Third Crusade, was unable to intervene himself, but he made his displeasure known when he heard of this terrible pogrom, and William Longchamp, the Justiciar, or Regent, dismissed the Sheriff and levied a fine on the city. Jews returned to York during the next fifty years and soon resumed their position in the commercial life of the city, until they were expelled, along with Jews throughout England, by Edward I in 1290.

Yorkshire barons were involved in the dynastic struggles in Scotland when in 1290 the Scottish throne became vacant following the death of Queen Margaret, the Maid of Norway. Two Yorkshire nobles, at different times in the 1290s during the reign of Edward I, were put in charge of Scotland – FitzAlan of Bedale and John, Earl of Richmond. York became the centre of government for England when the King moved north to deal with Wallace and Bruce. In 1300, while the Court was based in Yorkshire, the Queen gave birth to a son, Thomas of Brotherton, named after his birthplace.

Edward II presented his barons with two major problems. The first arose from his infatuation with a Gascon adventurer, Piers Gaveston, who until his execution in 1312 exercised a baleful influence over the King. The King gave several estates in Yorkshire to his favourite, including Knaresborough, Skipton, Holderness and Scarborough. Although excommunicated by the Church and twice forced into exile, Gaveston came to York in 1311 with the King. A group of barons, including the Percys, Cliffords and Warennes from Yorkshire, determined to remove Gaveston's evil influence. In 1312 the King and Gaveston fled to Newcastle, then travelled by sea to Scarborough, where the King went on to York, leaving his friend to defend Scarborough Castle. Gaveston was persuaded to leave Scarborough and was arrested and executed in 1312.

The second problem concerned the Scottish wars which continued during the reign of Edward II. In 1314 Edward's forces were ignominiously defeated at Bannockburn by Robert the Bruce; and Scottish forces, in alliance with the Earl of Lancaster, invaded Yorkshire. At Myton-on-Swale in 1319, in a battle in which a large number of clergy took part – hence the engagement was known as the Chapter (church meeting) of Myton – Edward was defeated. The King had a useful victory at Boroughbridge in March 1322, when Lancaster was taken prisoner along with Clifford and Mowbray. They were taken to Pontefract Castle, where they were tried for treason. Lancaster was beheaded outside the castle walls and the others were hanged in York. The Scots, however, remained in Yorkshire, pillaging and terrorising the countryside, although they were unable to take York or any of the major towns.

In October 1322 Robert the Bruce surprised and nearly caught the King, who was dining at Byland Abbey. Byland and Rievaulx Abbeys were looted and raids were made in the Vale of Pickering and in the East Riding. Ripon was set on fire by the main Scottish force, who returned home in October, but a section of their men wintered in Morley, until a truce was patched up which gave Yorkshire a respite. When the Scots later broke the truce, in 1327, the Court was again based in York, but Edward II had by then been deposed and later that year he was

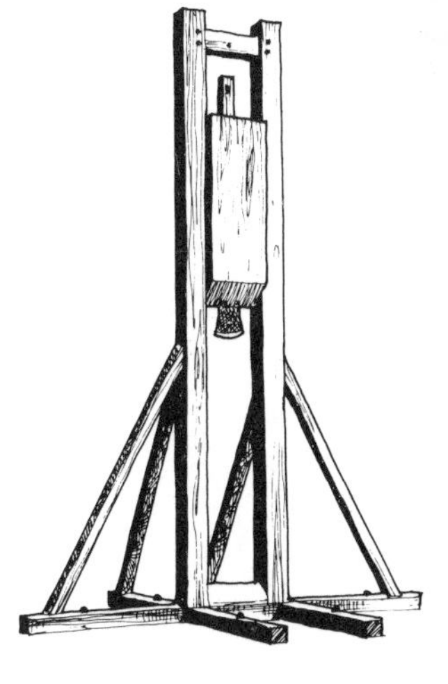

Halifax gibbet

Whitby market cross

murdered. Isabella, Edward's queen, became the real ruler, managing the affairs of state on behalf of her young son, Edward III, whose marriage to Philippa of Hainault Isabella arranged in York.

The last episode in the wars with the Scots in which Yorkshire was involved, before the country was ravaged by the Black Death, was an invasion begun by David II of Scotland, with French encouragement, in 1346. He reached the outskirts of York but was unable to take the city. Archbishop de la Zouche rallied the Yorkshiremen to resist, and, supported by the Percys, Nevilles and Mowbrays, inflicted a crushing defeat at Neville's Cross. David was imprisoned, first at Richmond, then at York, but was released in 1357 as part of a truce in the Hundred Years' War with the French.

The Black Death (a form of bubonic plague) hit Yorkshire in March 1349, decimating all classes from the nobility and clergy to the peasants. The great abbeys lost many of their inmates – eight out of ten from Meaux Abbey in Holderness, for example – and almost half the clergy in the West Riding perished. In the Deanery of Doncaster alone, two-thirds of the beneficed clergy died in 1349. In the rural areas there was a heavier rate of mortality in the more densely populated East Riding than in Cleveland, where direct contact between infected persons was less common in the scattered and isolated villages on the bleak uplands. Thus, whilst 21 per cent died in the deanery of Cleveland, there was a 61 per cent mortality in Dickering on the Wolds. In York, where the plague reached its height during the summer, a third of the population died, yet in 1377 the population of York was 50 per cent higher than in 1348. Although the Black Death undoubtedly contributed to the depopulation of many villages, recent researches have suggested that it merely accelerated a decline which had been taking place for most of the previous century. Pestilence and famine were fairly common in 14th-century England, and in Yorkshire the position was made worse by the endemic state of civil turmoil.

The really important part of north country history in the Middle Ages (from the Norman Conquest to Tudor times) is not, however, the perpetual bloodshed which took place between English and Scots. Much more important, even in the poor, barren and warlike north, is the story of art and civilisation. The most interesting record of this is to be seen in the architecture of the parish churches. Of some 11,000 ancient parish churches in England there are more than 600 in Yorkshire. These include fine examples of every one of the four medieval styles:

Later Romanesque (round arches)	1. Norman 1a. Transitional
Gothic (pointed arches)	2. Early English 3. Decorated 4. Perpendicular

Coverham church lych gate

There are also here and there odd survivals, usually mere fragments, of the Saxon (early Romanesque) architecture which was fashionable up to about 1050 in the south of England, and which remained so a little later in the north. Again, although Gothic architecture generally died out for a time in England after the Reformation, in the north there are interesting examples of good Gothic work as late as the mid-17th century.

Hooton Pagnell cross

There is a fair number of fragments of Saxon work-crosses, cross heads and hog-back stones in the North and West Ridings. Substantial pieces of Saxon work remain in the North Riding at Appleton-le-Street, Kirkby Hill, Kirkdale, Hovingham and Middleton; in the West Riding at Bardsey, Ledsham, Laughton-en-le-Morthen and Monk Fryston; in the East Riding at Skipwith and at Wharram-le-Street. At Ripon there is under the Minster a fine Saxon crypt, one of only six in England, and at Kirk Hammerton there is a complete Saxon church tower, chancel and nave, which now serves as a south aisle to the modern 19th-century church. York has fine examples of Saxon, as indeed of every other period of English church architecture, far too numerous to mention here.

Most of the interesting Yorkshire churches belong to medieval times, and their architecture is best studied having in mind the five classes or styles mentioned above. More than half the old Yorkshire churches show examples of Norman or Transitional Norman work. The Norman style is seen to great advantage in the churches of Adel and Birkin. There is fine Transitional Norman work in the chancel at Farnham and the tower at Riccall. The Early English style is exemplified in scores of churches, great and small. The whole eastern half of Beverley Minster, perhaps the loveliest church in Yorkshire, is Early English. Fine Decorated work is to be seen at Otley and at Skipton, in the lovely choirs at Ripon and Selby, and at its best in the superb church at Patrington. There are examples of Perpendicular work in almost every ancient church in the county; at the very least there are likely to be one or two windows in this style, inserted into earlier fabric. Most of the great town churches of the West Riding – Halifax, Rotherham, Sheffield and Wakefield – are mainly Perpendicular. There is a famous and very beautiful Perpendicular nave at Almondbury, near Huddersfield. The church of Thirsk is usually thought to be one of the best examples in Yorkshire of Perpendicular work. In every part of each of the three Ridings fine Perpendicular towers are a prominent feature of the landscape.

St James's chapel, east window

VIII Yorkists and Lancastrians

Red Rose of Lancashire

The dynastic quarrel between the Yorkists and Lancastrians for the throne of England was only one aspect of the dispute known as the Wars of the Roses, and it would be wrong to assume that Yorkshire was solid for those who bore the White Rose as their emblem, and that the people of Lancashire supported the Red Rose. This may be a convenient legend with which to add spice to present-day rivalries on the cricket field, but historically it is not well founded. In fact the Percys, the family of the Earl of Northumberland, were Lancastrians but they owned estates at Leconfield and Wressle in the East Riding, at Seamer and Topcliffe in the North Riding and at Spofforth in the West Riding.

The Cliffords of Skipton, who also owned a large part of Wharfedale, and the Talbots of Hallamshire were also Lancastrians. Much of the North Riding was owned by Yorkist families, the most powerful of these being the Nevilles of Middleham and Sheriff Hutton; the Scropes of Masham and Castle Bolton; and the Latimers of Danby, Snape and Well. Both the Scrope and Neville families had at different times in the 15th century occupied the Archbishopric of York, and one of the sons of Ralph Neville, the founder of the family fortunes, became Bishop of Durham. Inter-marriage amongst the numerous children of the great magnates resulted in family connections being forged between the houses of York and Lancaster, as when Ralph Neville took as his second wife a daughter of John of Gaunt, the head of the House of Lancaster, whilst one of his daughters married Richard, Duke of York, whose seat at Sandal Castle, near Wakefield, was a Yorkist stronghold. The ordinary people of Yorkshire – the yeoman farmers, the townsfolk and the rural labourers – had little choice but to follow the allegiance of their overlords, but for many of them the even tenor of their everyday lives was little disturbed by the Wars of the Roses.

White Rose of Yorkshire

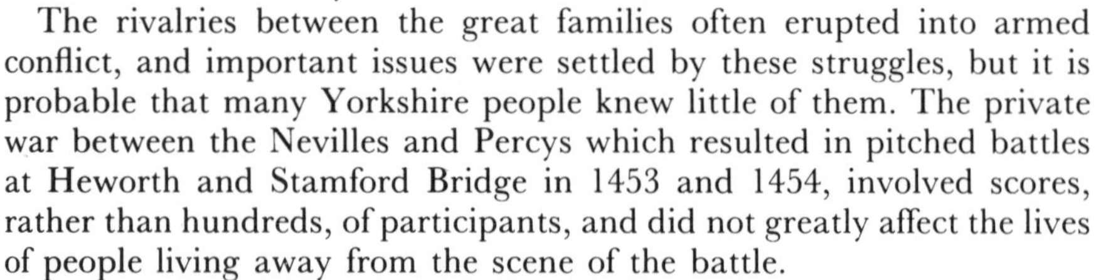

The rivalries between the great families often erupted into armed conflict, and important issues were settled by these struggles, but it is probable that many Yorkshire people knew little of them. The private war between the Nevilles and Percys which resulted in pitched battles at Heworth and Stamford Bridge in 1453 and 1454, involved scores, rather than hundreds, of participants, and did not greatly affect the lives of people living away from the scene of the battle.

The roots of the conflict go back into the 14th century and to the disputes which arose following the death of Edward III in 1377, after a reign of half a century. The throne passed to Richard II, who was then a young child, and the effective ruler was his uncle, John of Gaunt, Duke of Lancaster. On John of Gaunt's death in 1399, his oldest son, Henry, returned from exile, ostensibly to claim his inheritance. The welcome which he received, when he landed at Ravenser at the mouth of the Humber with Archbishop Arundel, persuaded him to go south to claim the crown from Richard who was then in Ireland. Richard was replaced by Henry IV and, after an attempt in 1400 to restore him, Richard was murdered in Pontefract Castle. The Percys, although nominally Lancastrians, like Henry, made several attempts to overthrow him. These events are the subject of Shakespeare's play, *Henry IV (Part 1)*, although historical accuracy gives way to dramatic licence in the account of the relations between Henry Percy (Hotspur), the King and Sir John Falstaff. Hotspur was slain at Shrewsbury in 1403, but his father, the Earl of Northumberland, organised another revolt in 1405, in which he was joined by Archbishop Scrope and the Earl of Mowbray. The rebellion was crushed at the Battle of Shipton Moor and Scrope was taken prisoner whilst discussing peace terms. After a brief trial Scrope had the dubious distinction of being the first archbishop to be executed for treason. Mowbray was also executed, but Northumberland escaped to lead another rising, which ended in his death on the field of battle at Bramham Moor, in 1408.

Henry IV died in 1413 and was succeeded by his son, as Henry V; and in 1422 by his grandson, Henry VI. (Henry was a favourite Lancastrian Christian name; Edward and Richard were preferred by the Yorkists.) The gains made by Henry V in France, including the famous victory at Agincourt in 1415, were lost during his son's reign (1422-1461). The incompetence and temporary insanity in 1453-4 of Henry VI gave his cousin, Richard, Duke of York, an opportunity to advance his claims to the throne. Richard was a grandson of Edward III's fifth son, Edmund, brother of John of Gaunt.

In 1455 a Yorkist army took possession of St Albans, captured the King and killed several Lancastrian nobles, including the Earl of Northumberland. This first battle of St Albans is generally regarded as marking the outbreak of the Wars of the Roses. The Yorkists, after this temporary success, were routed at Blore Heath, near Ludlow, in 1459, by a force which included many Yorkshiremen, recruited by the Earl of Salisbury. The Duke of York, together with Salisbury and his son, the Earl of Warwick, fled to Calais, which was then still under English control. The 'Calais Earls' regrouped their forces and invaded in 1460, defeating the King and taking him prisoner at the Battle of Northampton. Queen Margaret fled to Yorkshire and refused to accept the compromise known as the Act of Accord, under which York would become King on the death of Henry. The Queen wanted the throne for her infant son, Edward, born in 1453. In Yorkshire she raised an army of Lancastrians and in early December marched them from Hull to set up camp near

White lion of Mortimer

Black dragon of Ulster

Pontefract. Richard, Duke of York, travelled north with a force of 4,000 men, to his castle at Sandal, near Wakefield. The Lancastrians mustered five times that number. Richard's men, 'environed on every side, like fish in a net', were easily defeated at the Battle of Wakefield, 29 December 1460, and Richard himself was killed. His 18-year-old son, Edmund, Earl of Rutland, was killed in hand-to-hand combat by 'Butcher' Clifford, the lord of Skipton Castle. Richard's head was carried to the city of York, where, adorned with a paper crown, it was placed on a pole on Micklegate Bar. According to Shakespeare (*Henry VI, Part 3*, act 1, scene iv) Queen Margaret declared 'Off with his head, and set it on York gates; So York may overlook the town of York'. Many other Lancastrians who survived the battle were slaughtered, including the Earl of Salisbury, who was beheaded at Pontefract.

The Queen, at the head of the victorious Lancastrian army, its numbers swollen by marauding bands of Welsh and Scottish adventurers, headed south, where, to Margaret's dismay, they pillaged and looted as they advanced on London. At the second Battle of St Albans, 17 February 1461, Margaret's forces again defeated the Yorkists and also released the King. Reports of the barbarous behaviour of the Lancastrian forces stiffened the resistance of the Londoners, and Lord Mayor Lee broke off negotiations which he had begun to arrange for the admission of Margaret's forces to the city. Instead, he invited the Yorkists, led by the Earl of Warwick and Edward, Duke of York, son of the slaughtered Richard, to occupy London, where Edward was proclaimed King Edward IV. Margaret returned to Yorkshire, pursued by the Yorkists, who gathered recruits from all parts of southern England, the Midlands and East Anglia. At this time the Wars of the Roses appeared rather as a fight between north and south than one between Lancashire and Yorkshire, and Yorkshire was the stronghold of the Lancastrians!

In March 1461 the Yorkist forces, led by their King, Edward IV and by the Earl of Warwick, a Yorkshireman of the Neville family, advanced on Margaret's Lancastrians who were waiting near Tadcaster. For a time they were delayed by 'Butcher' Clifford's defence of the crossing of the River Aire, near Ferrybridge. Warwick succeeded in overcoming Clifford's resistance and forced his way through to Towton, on the main Doncaster to York road, where, on Palm Sunday, he met the Lancastrian forces and decisively defeated them. Clifford was killed during the retreat from Ferrybridge. Warwick is said to have killed his horse in the presence of his troops in a flamboyant gesture to demonstrate that he was willing to fight and die alongside his foot soldiers. This action had a tonic effect on the morale of the Yorkists, who fought like tigers to avenge their defeat at Wakefield. Cock Beck, which flows past the scene of the battle, ran red with the blood of the slaughtered Lancastrians and Yorkists, and when the Yorkists swept on to York, where Henry and Margaret were staying, they carried with them the heads of the Lancastrian barons. The heads of the Yorkists, still impaled on Mickle-

Falcon and fetterlock

gate Bar, were replaced with those of their enemies. The Battle of Towton was probably the bloodiest fought on English soil up to that time. The Yorkists mustered some 15,000 men, who were thrown against 20,000 Lancastrians, and the casualties amounted to about a quarter of those involved. It is said that the path of the retreating army could be traced all the way to York by the trail of bloodstains across the snow-covered Vale of York.

Although the 19-year-old Edward IV was crowned at Westminster Abbey in June 1461, the dynastic issue was far from settled. Margaret and Henry escaped from York and fled to Scotland, where, with help from the French and with the backing of the surviving Percys, who were still powerful in the north-east, they began to organise a Lancastrian revival. These efforts came to an end with Edward's victory at Hexham in 1464. Henry fled to Bolton-by-Bowland, near the Yorkshire-Lancashire border, where he was given refuge by Sir Ralph Pudsey. The church in Bolton contains a monument to Sir Ralph and to the 25 children whom he fathered by his three wives. In 1465 Henry moved in to Lancashire, where he was found wandering aimlessly. He was taken prisoner and on Edward's order was placed in the Tower of London.

New life was given to the Lancastrian cause, when Richard Neville, Earl of Warwick and one of the chief Yorkist supporters in Yorkshire, changed sides in 1470. The Nevilles of Middleham and Sheriff Hutton had been well rewarded for their contributions to the Yorkist party. Richard himself, known as the 'Kingmaker', had received a host of lucrative public offices from the grateful Edward IV: Admiral of England, Captain of Calais, Constable of Dover Castle and Lord Warden of the Cinque Ports, to name but a few. In addition to these prestigious posts Warwick was known to wield enormous influence over the King and was regarded by some foreign observers as the true ruler of England. His brother John was given the title and estates of the disgraced Earl of Northumberland, and therefore became inheritor of the power of the Percys in Northumberland and Yorkshire. Another brother, George, became Archbishop of York, as well as Chancellor of England.

The 'Kingmaker' was not satisfied with the trappings of office for himself and his family; he wanted power, not simply in Yorkshire and the north but also over the whole realm. When it became apparent that Edward had a mind of his own, and was not prepared to accept Neville's guidance, Warwick began to intrigue against his ruler.

Arms of the Savilles

The first sign of Edward's independence occurred as early as May 1464, when Edward secretly married Elizabeth Woodville, widow of a Lancastrian whose family had fallen on (comparatively) hard times and were determined to use marriage as a means of improving the family fortunes. Through the Woodvilles' marriages – Elizabeth had two sons by her former marriage and five brothers and six sisters – links were forged with other titled families, including William Herbert, the newly created Earl of Pembroke. Even Warwick's aunt, the 60-year-old Dowager Duchess of Norfolk, was cajoled into marrying the new Queen's teenage brother, John. These liaisons helped to create the nucleus of a court party which was outside the influence of the Nevilles. They also snapped up most of the eligible bachelors whom Warwick saw as possible husbands for his two daughters. The last straw came in 1467, when Edward allied himself to the Duke of Burgundy, and sealed the bargain by agreeing to the betrothal of his sister Margaret to the Burgundian ruler, Charles the Bold. Warwick had been working for an alliance with Louis XI of France who was the enemy of Charles. In the same year, Warwick's brother, Archbishop Neville, was dismissed as Chancellor of England, a clear sign that the influence of the Yorkshire family was on the wane.

Black Bull of Clarence

Warwick began in 1468 to intrigue with the King's older brother and then heir to the throne, George, Duke of Clarence. In July 1469 Warwick went to Calais for the wedding of his daughter Isabel to Clarence, the service being conducted by Archbishop Neville. Whilst they were away a rebellion began in the East Riding led by the mysterious Robin of Holderness, ostensibly to restore the Percys to their estates. Another of Warwick's brothers, who had replaced a Percy as Earl of Northumberland, was easily able to suppress it. Shortly afterwards another revolt broke out in Yorkshire, led by Robin of Redesdale – thought to be in fact Sir John Conyers of Hornby near Richmond, a relative of the Nevilles. Although the original rebels were mainly tenants of the Nevilles, other Yorkshire folk, who were dissatisfied with Edward's failure to bring peace and prosperity, joined in.

The Yorkshiremen gathered strength as they advanced south to meet the King's forces. At the same time Warwick and the newly-wed Clarence crossed from Calais, collected support in London and moved towards Banbury. Edward, deserted by many of his erstwhile supporters, was defeated at the Battle of Edgecoat, near Banbury and was taken prisoner. After a short period of incarceration in Warwick Castle Edward was sent to imprisonment in the Neville fortress of Middleham Castle. Warwick attempted to govern in the name of the imprisoned King, but within a few weeks a Lancastrian revolt on the Scottish borders forced him to release Edward, and a transparently unworkable display of amity between Warwick, Archbishop Neville and Clarence lasted only as long as the emergency. Edward, acting with a newly found sense of authority, successfully put down a rising in Lincolnshire in early March 1470 and then proceeded to York, where he denounced Warwick, Clarence and others as traitors. He pursued them to Exeter, averaging 16 miles a day in a forced march, a remarkable achievement at that time, but he arrived too late to prevent the traitors from fleeing to France.

Edward returned to Yorkshire during the summer to suppress a rebellion led by Lord Fitzhugh of Ravensworth, north of Richmond, and remained there whilst Warwick and Clarence plotted with their former Lancastrian enemy, ex-Queen Margaret, to effect a Lancastrian restoration. The bargain, achieved through the mediation of King Louis XI of France, ignored the claims of Clarence and envisaged the return of Henry VI. Inevitably, the agreement was sealed by another politically-inspired marriage, this time between Warwick's second daughter, Anne and Margaret's son, Edward, Prince of Wales.

In September, Warwick and a somewhat reluctant Clarence landed in Devon. Edward found himself isolated in Yorkshire and was unable to gather his forces to resist the invaders. He fled with some of his supporters to Holland, where they were sheltered by the Duke of Burgundy's governor, a representative of Edward's old ally and brother-in-law, the Duke of Burgundy. His wife, Elizabeth Woodville, took sanctuary in Westminster Abbey, where she bore a son, later to become Edward V.

Henry was released from prison and again became King of England, but he was back in the Tower six months later, and was murdered there in May 1471.

Edward landed with 1,500 supporters at Ravenspur, at the mouth of the Humber, where Henry IV had landed in 1399, but, unlike his predecessor, he found the people of Holderness unfriendly. The local people, led by the vicar of Keyingham and a local landowner, Martin de la Mare, on hearing that he was there merely to claim his family estates and not the crown, were eventually persuaded to allow him to spend the night at Kilnsea, 'a poore village, two miles from the place where he first set foot on land'. The next day he found the gates of Hull locked against him, but he had a more friendly reception at Beverley and York. He then went south to his family estates at Sandal, where he received only lukewarm support; even from his old ally, Lord Montagu of Pontefract, who was a Neville and, like his kinsman, Warwick, had changed his allegiance. Warwick, assuming that Montagu would deal with the threat which Edward's arrival posed, remained in the Midlands. Edward marched his men south, gathering support on the way, and bypassing Coventry, where Warwick was installed, made for London, where he was reunited with his wife and saw his infant son for the first time. Warwick met him at Barnet and was defeated and killed there on 14 April. Queen Margaret, who by this time had landed from France with her son, Edward, Prince of Wales, was defeated on 10 May at Tewkesbury, where the young Prince was killed. Margaret was later ransomed by Louis XI and returned to France. Edward entered London in triumph on 21 May, as the undisputed master of England, having probably ordered the killing of the unfortunate Henry.

That might have been the end of the Wars of the Roses, with the Lancastrian claimants and their chief supporters now dead and Queen Margaret a lonely exile. Many of the survivors changed sides when they saw the Lancastrian cause was lost, and those who did not lost their titles and estates to Yorkist supporters.

The Neville estates in Yorkshire passed to Richard, Duke of Glouces-

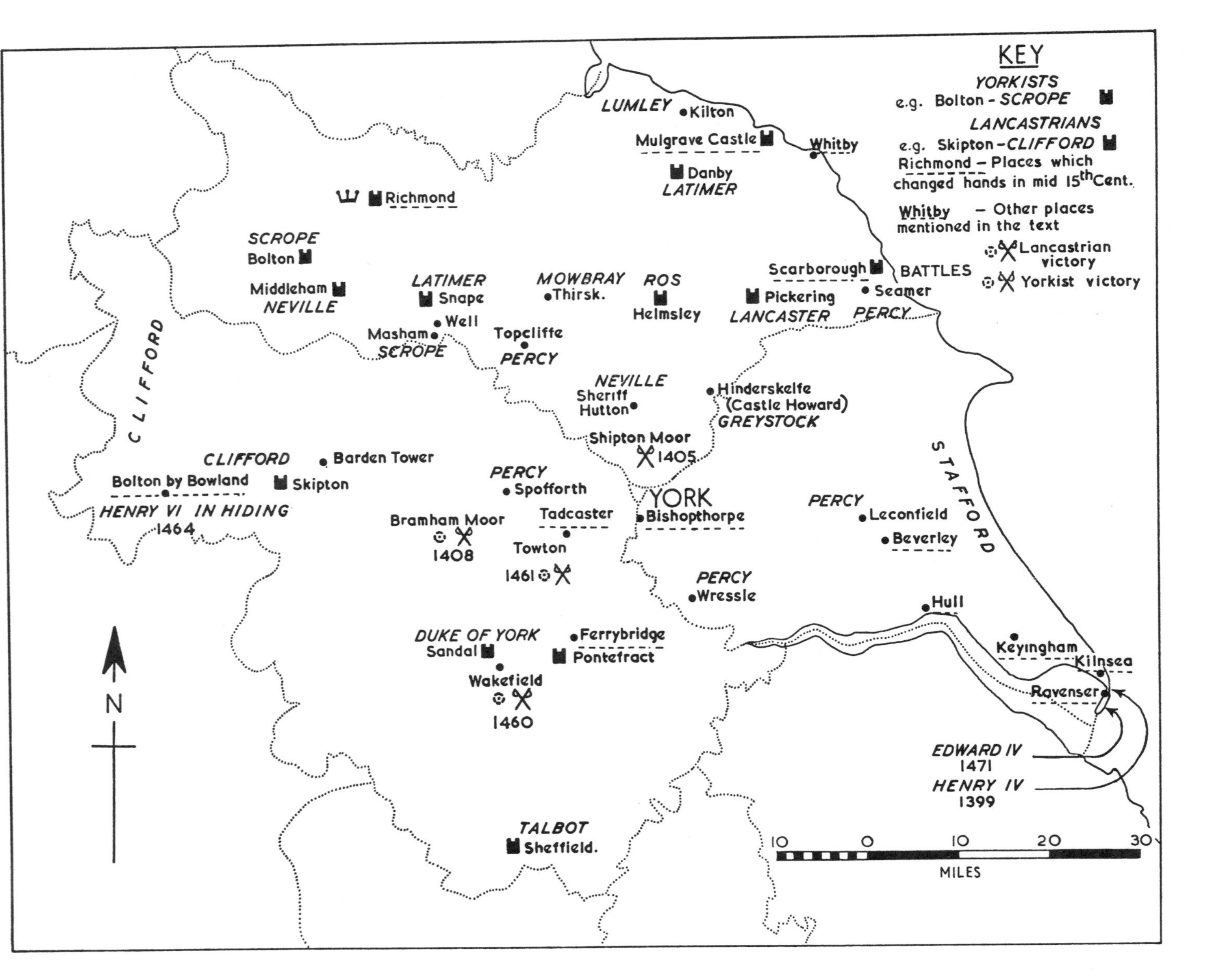

Map 6. Yorkists and Lancastrians.

ter, the King's brother and husband of Warwick's daughter, Anne Neville. The King's other brother, George, Duke of Clarence, who had adroitly changed sides in 1471, was pardoned, but was later put on trial and condemned as a traitor. In 1478 he died in the Tower, reputedly by being drowned in a butt of Malmsey wine. Edward was succeeded in 1483 by his young son, a boy of 10. Although he was proclaimed Edward V, he never had a chance to enjoy his royal status. After a struggle with the King's widow, Elizabeth Woodville, his uncle, Richard of Gloucester, was appointed Protector, to govern until Edward came of age. Richard had the King and his younger brother, the Duke of York, confined to the Tower. He certainly dethroned his nephew and had himself proclaimed King Richard III; and almost certainly had the two princes murdered. Richard had a short and violent reign. In 1485 Henry Tudor, a descendant of John of Gaunt through his mother, Margaret Beaufort, landed at Milford Haven and defeated and killed Richard at the Battle of Bosworth, 22 August 1485. Amongst the troops who fought for Richard were 80 men from York, a somewhat meagre contingent, considering the favours which Richard had bestowed on the city. Despite this lukewarm response, the city records recount that 'a great heaviness' fell upon the town on the news of their patron's death. Bosworth is usually taken as marking the end of the Wars of the Roses. Henry VII, the first of the Tudor kings, was a descendant in the female line of the Lancastrian, John of Gaunt. In 1485 he married Edward IV's daughter, Elizabeth, thus uniting the rival houses. To symbolise this union he took as his badge the Tudor rose, which combines the white rose of York and the red rose of Lancaster. Although during the first 15 years of his reign Yorkist claimants challenged Henry, by the time Henry VIII succeeded him in 1509, the succession was not in doubt.

Tudor Rose

One consequence of the turmoil and slaughter of the 30 years between the first Battle of St Albans (1455) and the Battle of Bosworth (1485) was to break the power and thin the ranks of the landed magnates whose rival ambitions had wreaked so much havoc. This was very obvious in Yorkshire, where the Percys, Cliffords, Nevilles and Scropes could no longer hold the country to ransom. Some of their estates were taken by the Crown (which explains why today Her Majesty the Queen, as Duke of Lancaster, is a major Yorkshire landowner) and others were passed to newly-ennobled subjects who were considered to be loyal to the Crown. Although the numbers killed were not large and the disruption to everyday life was much less than during the Civil War of the 17th century, a high proportion of those killed were members of the nobility. In over thirty years there were only 13 weeks of actual fighting, and more people died of plague than from battle wounds. The largest pitched battle was at Towton in 1461, and it was said that memories of this carnage discouraged Yorkshiremen from rallying to the support of Edward IV when he landed in 1471.

Towton Memorial

IX Yorkshire Monasteries

There were about seventy religious houses, or monasteries, in Yorkshire before the Reformation. These included abbeys, priories, nunneries and friaries, the chief of which are shown on map 7. The first great monastic order, the Benedictine, founded by St Benedict in A.D. 529, established Whitby Abbey in A.D. 657. This is the building associated with the great Abbess-Princess, St Hilda, and with Caedmon, the first English poet. The original building was destroyed by the Danes in A.D. 867, although some relics from it survive in the local museum near the abbey church. These include the tombstone of St Hilda's successor, Elfrida, daughter of King Oswy of Bernicia, who died in A.D. 714. Whitby's fate at the hands of the Danes was shared by other early foundations. A chronicler in 1069 wrote that there was then not a single monk left in Yorkshire. The present abbey ruins, which stand on the cliffs above Whitby, date from the first decade after the Norman Conquest, although building continued until the early 13th century.

Most of the Yorkshire monasteries whose traces survive today are foundations of the post-Conquest period, and belonged to religious orders which originated on the continent. At this time Christendom was an all-European concept, held together by a common allegiance to the Pope in Rome and a common language of devotion, Latin. Monks travelled freely from monasteries in France, Spain and Italy to found new communities in Britain. Often their motivation was a protest against the wealth, easy-going manners and ostentation of their brethren who had forgotten the vows of poverty, chastity and obedience which had been the guiding principles of the founders. Thus, the Cluniacs broke away from the Benedictines and established priories at Pontefract and Monk Bretton, and a nunnery at Arthington. The Cluniac houses were never completely independent of the parent Abbey of Cluny, in Burgundy, and were known as 'alien houses'. The Cluniacs soon came to outdistance their parents, the Benedictines, in wealth and splendour, and another reform movement, the Augustinians or Austin Canons (also known as Black Canons) was formed. They came to Yorkshire in the early 12th century and founded Nostell Priory (1113-14) and Bridlington Priory at about the same time. A few years later, in 1120, encouraged by Archbishop Thurston (1119-1140) they established a house at Embsay, near Skipton. In 1154 Alice de Romilly, the daughter of Cecily, who had first granted the site at Embsay, gave the canons a piece of land on a bend of the Wharfe at Bolton, where Bolton Priory was founded. During the next few decades Augustinian houses were established at Kirkham, Guisborough, Warter, Drax and Newburgh.

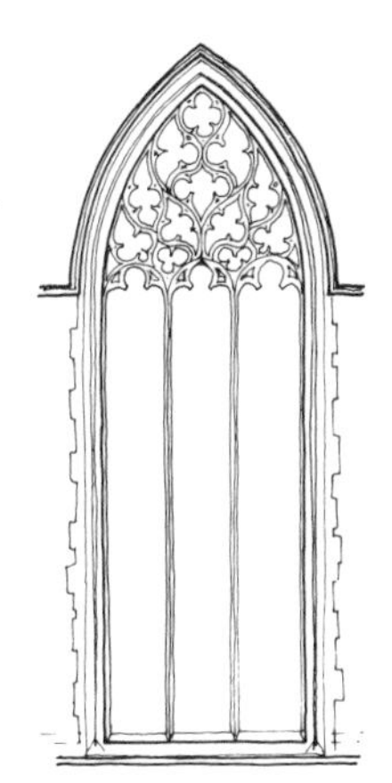
Decorated window, Bolton priory

The most important of the monastic reform movements was that of the Cistercians, like the Cluniacs an offshoot of the Benedictines, whose parent house at Cîteaux in Burgundy was founded in 1098. Every Cistercian house was independent, and was ruled by its own abbot. There were 20 of them in Yorkshire. Although, with a few exceptions, these were the richest of the Yorkshire monasteries, the monks who lived in them followed a simple, austere way of life. They did not concern themselves with study or scholarship, but believed in plain food and plenty of hard manual work on the land. When the Cistercian Order was spreading in England, monks of the other principal orders were already established on rich lands in the south of England. Partly for this reason, and partly because of their desire for a simple life, the Cistercians chose the fertile valleys amid the barren highlands of Yorkshire, far from the great centres of population. Because of their remoteness many of the Cistercian houses were spared the plundering which those of other orders suffered when local people used them as stone quarries. The ruins of the Yorkshire Cistercian houses are not only the most beautiful but are also the largest and most important monastic remains in England.

The Cistercians were, in a sense, puritanical, in that they distrusted colour and elaborate ornament. The new and very beautiful style of architecture, Early English, the style of the lancet arch, which developed in the 13th century, fitted in very well with their ideas. Many of the Yorkshire houses include beautiful examples of this style. The great Yorkshire Cistercian monastic houses were Rievaulx, Fountains, Jervaulx, Meaux, Kirkstall, Roche and Sawley, all founded 1131-1150. Nowhere else in England is there anything quite like this group of Cistercian houses. Kirkstall Abbey was founded by Henry de Lacy, grandson of the Ilbert de Lacy who had been granted land in Skyrack Wapentake by the Conqueror. Fountains originated from a dispute amongst monks in the Benedictine abbey of St Mary's in York, one of the richest of the Yorkshire houses, whose Abbot was a great prince of the Church. He was a mitred abbot – i.e. the Pope had granted him the privilege of wearing a bishop's mitre – and he was later summoned regularly to sit in the House of Lords, along with the Abbot of Selby.

Doorway, Jervaulx

About 1130 a group of monks living in St Mary's became dissatisfied with the slackness and negligence which they found around them. The idea of reform was gaining ground and it was said that at the newly founded Cistercian Abbey of Rievaulx monks were living as they really should. So 13 of the monks, led by one known as Richard the Prior, attempted to improve the discipline of their own house. They soon came into conflict with Abbot Geoffrey and called on Archbishop Thurstan to investigate their complaints. This made Geoffrey more angry than

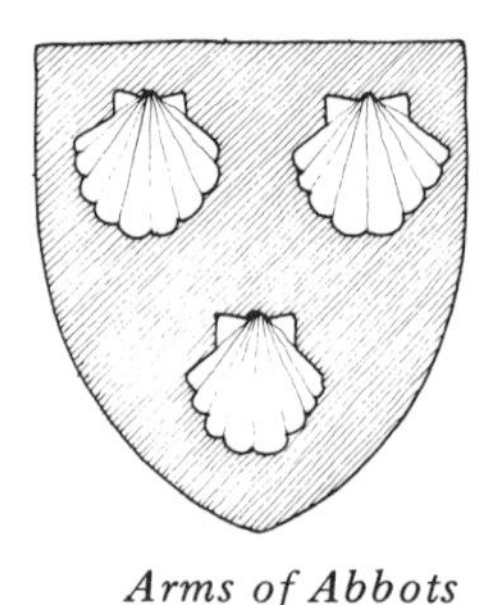

Arms of Abbots of Jervaulx

ever, and when the Archbishop paid a visit there was a tremendous tumult in the chapter house, and Thurstan, with Richard and his friends, had to seek refuge in the church. When Thurstan managed to get away he took the 13 with him, and for three months they lived in his palace. All save one ('whose belly clave to the ground') refused to make terms with the Abbot, and finally the remaining 12, with one more recruit, after spending Christmas Day with the Archbishop at Ripon, went out on the next day – the Feast of St Stephen – along the River Skell. Here, three miles away, the Archbishop gave them a site on which to build a new monastery of their own. Richard was elected Abbot. He and his monks suffered many privations – in a time of famine they had to eat herbs and leaves – but they survived and established a monastery which became, perhaps, the most famous of all the Yorkshire religious houses.

However, Fountains, like many other abbeys, as it prospered lost many of its early ideals. We learn much of the state of religious houses from the reports of 'Visitations' made by the church authorities. Sometimes the charges were trifling. Thus the nuns of Nun Appleton occasionally left their nunnery to visit the local alehouse. (Yorkshire villages with names with Monk or Nun in them are usually the sites of former religious houses. Examples include Nun Appleton, Nun Monkton, Monk Bretton, etc. The canons of Warter had been sleeping off the premises, and wearing gold and silver rings. At Egglestone the brethren were 'full of quarrelling among themselves'.

In 1321 the extravagance of the canons was castigated by Archbishop Melton and the Prior was ordered 'to abide, like a careful shepherd, in the place where he bears rule, without gadding here and there'. There were graver charges of loose living and indiscipline against the nuns of Basedale, the Abbot of Coverham and the Abbot and some of the brethren in York St Mary's. On the other hand, the nuns at Arthington were praised as 'being of the good life'.

Attempts at religious reform did not always lead to the establishment of new monastic orders, and to the building of monasteries which in due course became centres of wealth and power. Some dissidents became mendicant friars, living simply, begging for alms and ministering to the poor and the sick. The best known of the mendicant friars were the Franciscans, or Grey Friars, who came to Yorkshire in 1258 at the invitation of Ralph FitzRandal, Lord of Middleham. He settled them on a site outside the walls of Richmond, where they built a simple church. Although they later enlarged the church and added other buildings, they never aspired to the magnificence of the monastic orders. The last addition to the Richmond Friary was a bell tower, which was finished towards the end of the 15th century, about fifty years before the Order was suppressed by Henry VIII. The Franciscans built friaries and churches at Beverley, Doncaster, York and Scarborough. Five other orders of mendicant friars operated in Yorkshire between the 13th and 16th centuries. The best known were the Dominicans (Black Friars) and

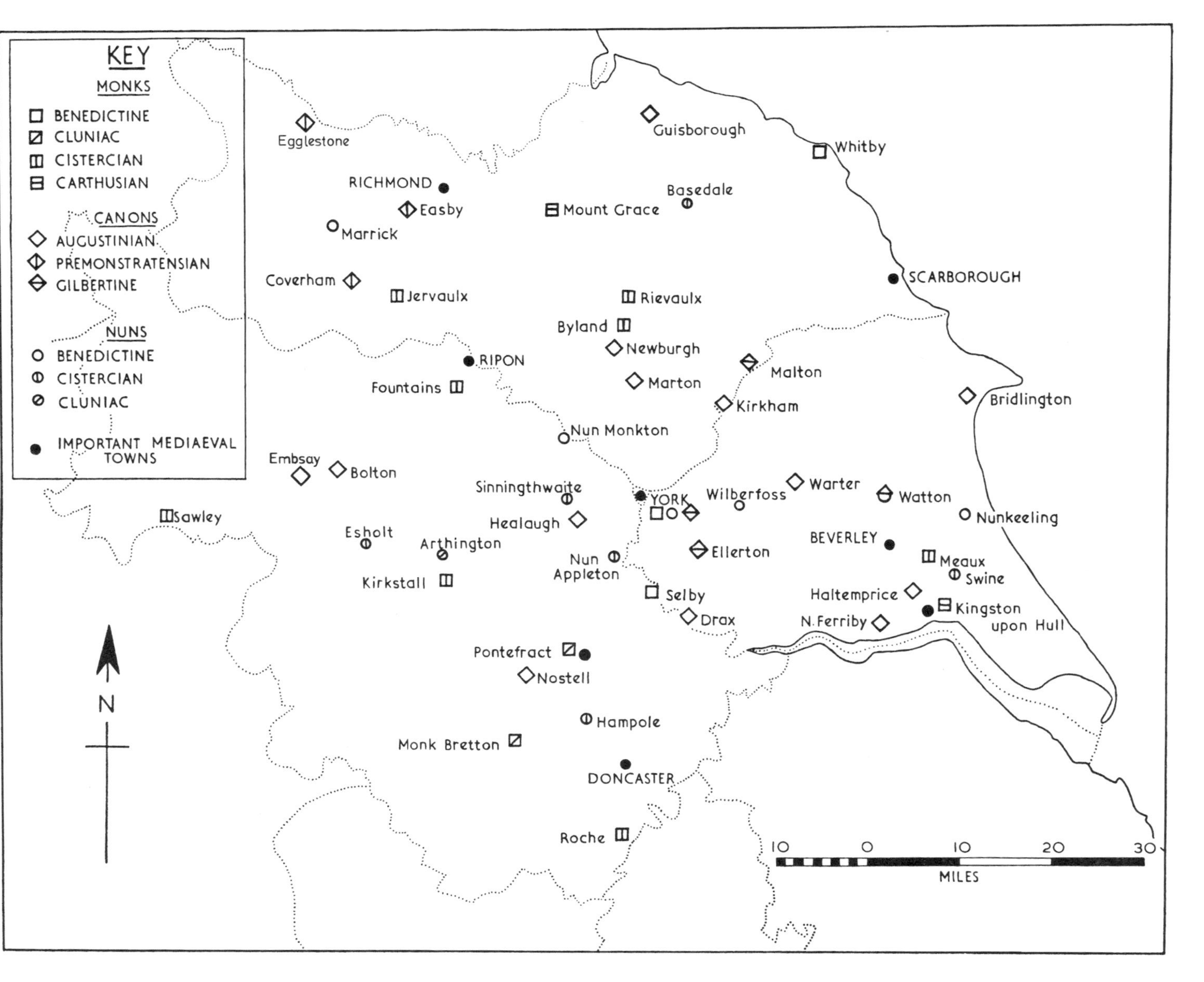

Map 7. Some Yorkshire Monasteries.

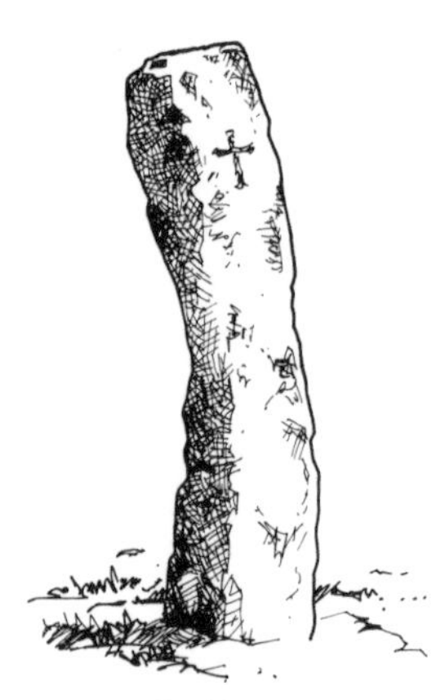

Guide post on Monk's Way

the Carmelites (White Friars). Whitefriar Gate in Hull and the Friarage Hospital at Northallerton are reminders of their presence.

Another reform movement which influenced the religious and social life of Yorkshire in the 14th century was that inspired by John Wycliffe, who was born at Hipswell, near Richmond, in 1320. Wycliffe translated the Bible into English, and advocated radical egalitarian ideas. He was judged a heretic in 1382, for his views on the doctrine of transubstantiation. His followers, known as Lollards, were involved in the Peasants' Revolt of 1381, which drew in a number of Yorkshire barons – including Nevilles and Cliffords – and there were disturbances in York, Beverley, Scarborough and Pontefract. These towns were heavily fined when the revolt was suppressed. These events, however, were less to do with religion than with the political struggles against the power of John of Gaunt. Wycliffe's religious ideas survived his death in 1384 and influenced the course of the Reformation during the next century.

The monasteries were an important element in the social life of rural Yorkshire. They encouraged sheep farming in the Yorkshire Dales – Fountains Fell, above Malham, for example, provided grazing land for sheep from Fountains Abbey, which were brought along some 25 miles of green tracks. Bolton Priory, one of the smaller houses, probably employed over 200 craftsmen, shepherds, foresters, etc., in addition to the monks. In addition to their economic activities the monastic houses provided the rudiments of a welfare state for the poor of their districts.

However, the King was determined to destroy the monasteries, partly because he saw them as centres of Papal influence, and partly because he felt that their wealth could be put to better use. The smaller houses were dissolved in 1536, and the larger ones in 1539. Their treasures were confiscated by the King; their estates were granted or sold to his courtiers; and their houses and churches were torn down or allowed to decay, or were converted into mansions for the new Tudor nobles.

For two and a half centuries there were, or were supposed to be, no monks, canons or nuns in Yorkshire. In fact, Bar Convent at York was founded in 1686, less than a century and a half after Henry's dissolution of all the religious houses of Yorkshire. However, Bar Convent contrived to exist only by remaining very quiet and inconspicuous. Its neighbours were never quite sure whether it was a nunnery or only a boarding school for young ladies. It was not until 1829 that English Roman Catholics were given the same liberties as their Protestant fellow subjects (though various of their disabilities had been removed by a series of 'emancipation' Acts, dating from one brought in by a great Yorkshireman, Sir George Savile, in 1778). After the outbreak of the French Revolution (1789-1793) the exiled French monks and nuns – like other French exiles – were welcomed in England. A group of them came to Haggerston, Northumberland, in 1795, and removed to Scorton in Yorkshire in 1807. The monastery of St John of God is still there, where it manages a hospital for 150 incurably sick men. Apart from Bar Convent, this was the first monastic house of any kind to be set up in Yorkshire after the great dissolutions of 1536 and 1539.

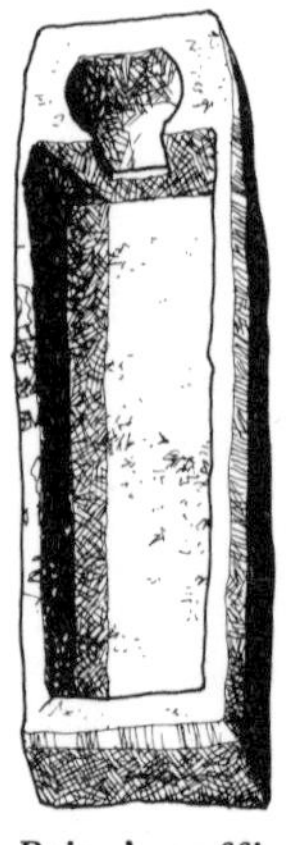

Prior's coffin

X The Reformation in Yorkshire

Brass of Thomas Tonge

Although Yorkshire people made great contributions to the Reformation – for example, the work of Wycliffe and the Lollards and of Miles Coverdale – there was widespread dissatisfaction with the dissolution of the monasteries by Henry VIII in 1536 and 1539. Even though some of them were not well managed, the monasteries were less unpopular in Yorkshire than in some other parts of England, and the Reformation was less welcome. Support for the traditional Roman Catholic form of Christianity was strong in Yorkshire, despite the fact that Cardinal Wolsey, who led the harassment of the monasteries during the 1520s, was Archbishop of York from 1514 until his fall in 1530. Many members of the Yorkshire clergy and nobility regarded the attacks on the monasteries, which culminated in their dissolution, as being acts inspired by the doctrines of Martin Luther; although the King remained a nominal Catholic, and had actually been called 'Defender of the Faith' by Pope Leo X in 1521 for his writings against Luther. Religious feelings were closely bound up with political sentiments, and one of the issues which concerned Yorkshire folk was the centralisation in London of financial and political power which had been growing under Wolsey and his successor, Thomas Cromwell. This process went back to the reign of Henry VIII's father, Henry VII, who had broken the remaining powers of the great Yorkshire magnates, partly by burdening them with heavy taxes and partly by forcing them to bear the cost of maintaining royal visits to the county. The Percys, for example, were ordered to pay the costs of the magnificent burial service held at the King's command in Beverley Minster in 1489 for the murdered Earl of Northumberland. They were further impoverished in 1503 by being forced to support the retinue of Princess Margaret during her progress through Yorkshire on her way to marry James IV of Scotland.

The religious and political discontents came to a head during the reign of Henry VIII. The immediate cause was the controversy over Henry's decision to divorce Catharine of Aragon in 1530, and the subsequent declaration that Henry was 'supreme Head of the Church'. There was the threat of a rising in Yorkshire: 'York will be in London hastily'. Unrest grew with the suppression of the smaller monasteries in 1536. A few monasteries, such as the Austin Priory at Guisborough, had been active in the education of young Yorkshiremen, and the nunneries (of which Wilberfoss and Esholt were outstanding) had provided the

Pilgrimage of Grace badge

only education open to girls of gentle birth. The close involvement of the monasteries in the social and economic life of the county had built up a fund of goodwill amongst their neighbours.

In 1536 a rising, known as the Pilgrimage of Grace, began in Lincolnshire and soon spread to Yorkshire. Robert Aske, a lawyer whose family lived at Aughton in the Derwent Valley, was persuaded to lead the rebels. He received enthusiastic support from the populace in York, Hull and Halifax, but many of the gentry and nobility hesitated. Archbishop Lee of York and the King's general, Lord Darcy of Templehurst, took refuge in Pontefract Castle, hoping to avoid involvement, but they were eventually persuaded to join forces with Aske. Soon other waverers were brought in, and eventually the list of supporters read like a roll-call of the Yorkshire gentry, with names such as Percy, Scrope, Fairfax, Lumley, Neville, Conyers and Norton amongst them. Of course, the rebels could count on the support of the abbots and priors of the surviving monasteries, like Fountains, Jervaulx and Bridlington.

Hull surrendered and then the rebels marched on Doncaster. By this time, only three great Yorkshire families were still loyal to the King, and only one major Yorkshire castle was in the hands of the loyalists – the stronghold of Skipton, belonging to the Cliffords. The leaders of the two armies met on Doncaster bridge, and the Duke of Norfolk, in the Kings's name, promised Aske (if he would disband his army) a free pardon, and a parliament, to meet at York (though he was careful not to promise the restoration of their property to the monks). So the rebels tore off their badges showing the Five Wounds of Our Lord, and swore they would now wear no badge but the King's. Whether or not the King intended to keep his promises no-one knows. Anyhow, a further outbreak of violence gave him a good excuse for breaking them. The rising was put down, and Aske was drawn on a hurdle through the streets of York, then hanged in chains on a turret of the castle.

The King had already ordered that any monks who gave trouble should be 'tied up without further delay or ceremony'. Various abbots and priors who were, or were supposed to have been ringleaders in the revolt were to be executed. The abbots of Fountains and of Jervaulx, the prior of Bridlington, the ex-abbot of Rievaulx and the ex-prior of Guisborough were, in fact, hanged, some at Tyburn, some in Lancaster. When the second wave of dissolution came in 1539, monks and canons went quietly, drew their pensions and accepted the new order of things. Henry's savage lesson in 1537 had been sufficient. Prior Moone of Bolton, for example, signed the deed of surrender along with 14 of the surviving brethren. He received a pension of £40 per annum and the others received smaller payments. Five canons from Bolton were allowed to retain the livings of village churches in the Craven district which had previously belonged to the Priory. The priory church was spared the destruction which was visited on the other buildings, and was able to continue as a place of worship for the local villagers, as a chapelry

8. (*above*) St John the Baptist, Adel, near Leeds, one of the best examples of a Norman village church in Yorkshire.

9. (*below*) Ripon Minster and the river Skell. The original church was founded in A.D. 660. The present church, which became a cathedral in 1836, includes a mixture of styles including Norman, Early English and Perpendicular.

10. Skipton Castle, the stronghold of the Cliffords. The early 14th-century round tower was built in the time of Robert de Clifford.

11. Micklegate Bar, York, originally Norman, but on the site of a Roman gateway.

12. North Bar, Beverley, *c.* 1409, a fine example of early 15th-century brickwork.

13. (*above*) Selby Abbey, started by Benedictines under Abbot Hugh de Lacy about 1100 and restored after the collapse of the central tower in 1690 and a fire in 1906.

14. (*below*) St Mary's, York, a Benedictine foundation started in the reign of William Rufus on the site of an Anglo-Saxon abbey.

15. Nostell Priory, an 18th-century country house built for Sir Rowland Winn on the site of a 12th-century Augustinian priory.

16. St Peter's church, Howden, framed by its own ruins, following the collapse of the choir in 1696.

subordinate to Skipton. It serves as the parish church of Bolton Abbey to the present day.

Although Yorkshire was thought to be staunchly Roman Catholic, it produced two important scholars of the Protestant Reformation. Wycliffe and his Lollards have already been referred to. The other was Miles Coverdale, who took his name from the valley of that name in Wensleydale. He was responsible for a new translation of the Bible in 1526. The idea that people should be able to read the Scriptures in their own language rather than in Latin was an essential tenet of the new Protestantism which emanated from Luther, and which challenged the right of the Church to be the sole intermediary between man and his Maker.

When Henry was succeeded in 1547 by his son, King Edward VI, it was clear that the Reformation movement would go further still, for Henry himself had lived and died a Catholic, though not a very loyal one. However, Edward and the ministers who would have governed for him (for he was only a boy) were mainly convinced Protestants, hating the Pope and all he stood for. There was then no chance of the monasteries being set up again. Indeed, in Edward's reign the Reformation, which had already wrecked the monasteries, now went on to affect the parish churches. They were not, of course, destroyed, but they lost many of their treasures, their fine embroidered vestments, often all but one of their bells, and much of their lovely altar plate –silver or even gold, ornamented with precious jewels. The Communion Service (which was to replace the Mass) needed few ornaments of any kind, and the government could do with all the treasure it could lay its hands on for financing its wars with the Scots.

In the west there was a tremendous uproar about all this, but there was little sign as yet of rebellion in Yorkshire and the north (still, perhaps, remembering the executions after the Pilgrimage of Grace) except at Seamer, near Scarborough. This was a riot, rather than a rebellion, led by the parish clerk and supported by the other villagers, who were mostly tenants of the Percys. Thomas Percy, the 7th Earl of Northumberland, was a whole-hearted Roman Catholic. Moreover he had his father's death to avenge for Sir Thomas, his father, had been executed at Tyburn in 1537, after the failure of the Pilgrimage of Grace. When Edward was followed by his Catholic sister Mary, she undid the work of the Reformation as far as she dared (and seriously thought of moving her capital from Protestant London to Catholic York, after she had earned the hatred of the Londoners). However, despite her wishes, she was able to do very little in the way of restoring the monasteries. After 1558 when she died and was succeeded by her half-sister, Elizabeth I, there was no hope whatever of this. Like her father, Elizabeth would have no Pope challenging her authority in England, and in any case by this time the property of the monasteries had been very widely distributed among her courtiers. They would never willingly give it up.

The northern nobles and gentlemen who had shared Mary's religious opinions were soon plotting against her half-sister, Elizabeth. The younger Percy, Henry, was loyal, at any rate at first, but his brother Thomas was not. The north was, however, fairly quiet until Mary, Queen of Scots, a Catholic and a strong claimant to the English throne, came to England in 1568. Thenceforward she was the centre of constant Catholic plots. In 1569 the Percys, in firm alliance with the Nevilles, broke out into open revolt.

They took Durham, had Mass said in the Minster, trampled on the English Prayer Book and broke up the wooden communion table which had replaced the old stone altar. They then took Ripon and had Mass said in the Minster there. Next, their plan was to capture York, and from there to organise a flying column to rush down to Tutbury, where Mary was imprisoned, and set her free to marry the Duke of Norfolk, the richest man in England, the only English duke and, though perhaps not then a declared Catholic, the head of what is to this day the leading English Catholic family. They could not, however, take York without more artillery, and they suddenly changed their plans and retreated into County Durham. The Revolt of the Northern Earls – the Rising of the North – was over.

There is an Elizabethan ballad, 'The Rising in the North', to be found in any good ballad collection, which gives some picturesque local details. The rebels are referred to by the names of the badges (not usually coats of arms) on their banners. The Dun Bull is Neville, the Half Moon is the Percys' silver crescent, the 'three doggs with golden collars' (the Three Greyhounds) seem to be the arms (not badge) of the Mauleverer family. All these are to be seen in Yorkshire today, in church buildings, monuments and windows, and very often in inn signs.

Though the Percys were the most famous family involved in the rebellion, the Nortons of Norton Conyers are perhaps the most interesting. There is a thrilling story told of how old Richard Norton (who had been in arms in the Pilgrimage of Grace in 1536), although he was a grey-bearded old man, rode out to battle at the head of eight of his nine sons, and risked and lost all for the sake of his Queen (Mary) and his Catholic faith. Actually he had 11 sons, not nine, and two of them did not take part in the rebellion. Of those who did, not all were executed. (Nor was old Richard, for he escaped safely overseas.) One of Wordsworth's best poems is about it – 'The White Doe of Rylstone'. The Nortons rode, as Richard had done in 1536, under a banner showing the Cross and the Five Wounds of Our Lord. It was this banner, embroidered by his daughter, which in Wordsworth's version of the story the dying Norton begged his last remaining son to carry through the Queen's forces and to lay on the ruined altar of Bolton Priory. In placing it there he also was slain, and there his sister, coming to meet him, found instead a newly-made grave.

When the revolt collapsed, some of the Nortons were taken prisoner, tried for treason and executed. Neville escaped to Flanders and lived there on a pension given to him by England's deadly enemy, the King of Spain. Percy fled over the Border into Scotland, where his first hosts, although they were border robbers and bitter enemies of the Percys, refused to give him up. In 1572 the Scottish Douglases sold him to Elizabeth for £2,000. He was beheaded at York, in the 'Pavement' (the market-place). With his last breath he declared his Catholic faith and boasted proudly, 'I am a Percy, in life and death'. His head was placed on a pole on Micklegate Bar. With him on the scaffold he had his greatest treasure, given to him by Queen Mary, a gold cross, in which was set a thorn said to be from Our Lord's Crown of Thorns. (This relic is still preserved in the famous Roman Catholic school, Ampleforth College.)

This was the last Percy rebellion. However, it was not the end of Catholic plots, or of trouble with the Percys. Elizabeth was now firm on her throne. Foreign support of her rebellious subjects naturally enough made her more popular than ever. Indeed, although Acts of Parliament were passed, punishing Catholics merely for being Catholics, the majority of the Protestants remained loyal to her. In any case, by this time she had established a very efficient secret service, through which she knew all about plots almost as soon as the plotters had met. She had very little serious trouble with Yorkshire in her later years, and when she died in 1603 it seemed as if the North was quiet at last. Then, only two years after she had been followed by her chosen successor, James I, son of her old enemy Mary Queen of Scots, there was yet another Catholic plot. As usual, the Percys were involved. The leader was another Yorkshireman, Guy Fawkes (an old boy of St Peter's School, York). Of the 13 chief conspirators, four or possibly five were old boys of St Peter's School. Five more had Yorkshire associations of one kind or another. Henry, the ninth Earl of Northumberland, had no great taste for politics, but his second cousin, Thomas Percy, was a born conspirator. It was Percy who actually hired the house next door to Parliament and installed Guy Fawkes in it as his servant, John Johnson. After Parliament had been blown up there was to have been a great Catholic rebellion. When the revolt came, Percy was to supply the rebels at Doncaster with 10 galloping horses from the Earl's stables and £4,000 of the Earl's rents to help the revolt. Of course the rebellion never came. Percy was killed resisting arrest; the Earl was shut up in the Tower from 1605 to 1621; and Guy Fawkes was tortured and finally executed.

Arms of Hull

From then onwards neither Yorkshire nor the Percys were seriously involved in later Catholic plots.

XI Yorkshire in the Civil War

Yorkshire was deeply involved in the Civil War, which is generally regarded as having begun in 1642, when Charles I left London and set up his standard at Nottingham, and as having ended with the beheading of the King 30 January 1649. However, its causes go back for at least a generation before 1642 and the issues which were raised by the conflict were not resolved until the accession of William and Mary, 40 years after the death of Charles. The constitutional issue centred on the right of the King to rule without consulting Parliament. As Thomas Stockdale of Bilton near Harrogate put it, should monarchs be entitled to rule 'according to their own fancies, or their flattering favourites' malevolent affections'? Closely interlocked with this were economic questions concerning taxation, the granting of commercial monopolies, and the disposal by the monarch of profitable public offices; and, equally important, the rights and privileges of the Church and the freedom of citizens to worship in ways which might not be approved of by the King. The conflict between King and Parliament appeared during the reign of James I (1603-1625) but did not threaten the peace of the realm until Charles I encountered resistance to his efforts to persuade Parliament to levy taxes to support his military expenditure. In 1637 the Scots – over whom the English King had exercised authority since James VI of Scotland came to the English throne as James I – resisted Charles's attempt to introduce a new prayer book, and in 1638 further evidence of Scottish resistance was demonstrated by the drawing up of a National Covenant and the abolition of the episcopate by a church assembly in Glasgow.

The first Bishops' War, between Charles and the Scots, broke out in 1639, and was ended in June by the Treaty of Berwick, but in the following year a second Bishops' War ended with a Scottish victory at the Battle of Newburn. Charles was forced to sign the Pacification of Ripon, which was later replaced by a permanent treaty, safeguarding the rights of the Presbyterian Church in Scotland.

One of the leading figures in the King's service at this time was Thomas Wentworth, who became Earl of Strafford in 1640. Wentworth, who was one of the richest men in England, took his title from the wapentake of Strafford, in south Yorkshire where his great country house, Wentworth Woodhouse, was situated. He had built up a large following amongst the gentry in the Sheffield area, by his ability to dispense patronage through the various offices which he held, which included those of the Lord President of the Council of the North and the Lord Deputy of Ireland. His followers included Thomas Edmunds of Worsborough, Sir Richard Scott of Barnes Hall and Sir Edward Osborne of Thorpe Salvin. The people of Sheffield itself, like those of most of the Yorkshire towns, inclined to the parliamentary side in the Civil War, however, although after the capture of Sheffield Castle in 1643 by royalist troops under the Earl of Newcastle, the Sheffield iron foundries were making cannon for the King's army.

Coley Hall gatehouse

The King's difficulties with the Scots forced him to summon Parliament in 1640. He did so on the advice of Wentworth, who had recently been ennobled, and who had become the King's right-hand man. The Short Parliament, which lasted from 13 April to 3 May, refused to grant Charles money until their grievances should be redressed. The King dissolved Parliament and called a Great Council in York, at which many of the Yorkshire gentry attended. They refused to grant him the funds he needed and recommended the summoning of another Parliament – the Long Parliament, which sat from November 1640 until the outbreak of the Civil War in 1642. One of its first acts was to impeach Strafford and the Archbishop of Canterbury, William Laud. Laud and his supporter, Richard Neile, Archbishop of York, had incurred the wrath of the many Puritan clergy and gentry in Yorkshire by introducing what they regarded as 'Papist' rituals and ornaments in the Church of England. Sir Henry Slingsby of Scriven wrote in his diary that he thought 'it came too near to idolatory to adorn a place with rich cloaths and other furniture'. In 1641 Strafford's impeachment was changed into a bill of attainder and in May he was executed. Laud met a similar fate in 1645. Strafford's tomb can be seen at Wentworth Woodhouse.

The Long Parliament also passed a number of Acts in 1641 which struck at the arbitrary system of government which Charles, aided by Strafford and Laud, had introduced. For example, both the Star Chamber and the Council of the North were abolished. The citizens of York were not pleased by the abolition of the Council of the North, which had been based in the city and which had brought with it some honour and much wealth. When the King visited the city on his way south from Scotland in June he was presented with a petition, asking for the restoration of the Council. Although he was not able to do so, he found it possible to reject the Nineteen Propositions which were put to him by Parliament during his stay in York. In March 1642 the King was again in York, where, for four months, he established his headquarters at Sir Arthur Ingram's house, and attempted to win Yorkshire over to his cause. The control of Hull was perceived by both King and Parliament to be of crucial importance. A large store of arms and provisions, which had been accumulated in support of the earlier Scottish campaigns, remained in Hull, and the port itself also afforded an opportunity for contact by sea with London and across the North Sea to Holland, where

Queen Henrietta Maria was gathering support for the King. Parliament appointed Sir John Hotham as governor, but the King nominated the Earl of Newcastle. Hotham took up his post before the Earl could reach Hull. In April 1642 the King, with a troop of 300 horse, travelled from York to demand admission to the city. According to Hotham's own account, the governor went to the gates, fell upon his knees before the King and told him, 'I had had that place delivered me under that sacred name of trust. I could not satisfy him . . . without incurring to me and my posterity the odious name of villain and faith-breaker'. Charles was forced to return to York, denouncing Hotham as a traitor. In fact, Hotham did change sides, and was later executed in 1645, but Hull remained loyal to the parliamentary cause.

Two months later the King again advanced on Hull but was halted near Beverley, when men from Hull opened the sluices on the river and flooded the countryside. The King, who was almost captured, was again forced to retreat. The stores in Hull were sent to London, to be available to the parliamentary forces there. However, the King was able to acquire a shipload of arms and other supplies which were sent up the Humber from Holland by the Queen. A meeting of Yorkshire gentry on Heworth Moor, reputedly attended by 40,000, was a final attempt to rally Yorkshire to the royalist side. Many of those present signed a petition, praying that King and Parliament should be reconciled, which Thomas Fairfax attached to the saddle of the King's horse. It has been estimated that in 1642 242 Yorkshire families supported the King; 128 were parliamentarians; 69 were either divided in their loyalties or changed sides during the war; and 240 did not declare allegiance to either side. The leader of the parliamentary forces was Ferdinando, Lord Fairfax of Denton and Nun Appleton, ably supported by his son Thomas (Black Tom); the King chose a Clifford, the Earl of Cumberland, as his standard bearer in Yorkshire. After initial royalist reverses, Cumberland was replaced by the Earl of Newcastle. Unlike the position during the Wars of the Roses, on this occasion the Percys and the Cliffords were on opposite sides. Northumberland, the head of the Percy family, threw his support on the side of Parliament. The sympathies of the clothing towns (Bradford, Halifax, Leeds, Dewsbury, Wakefield) were mainly with Parliament.

The rejection by the King of the Nineteen Propositions, put to him in York by Parliament, was the signal for the Civil War to commence. The King rode to Nottingham, where he raised his standard on 22 August and rallied those loyal to him for support in resisting the demands of Parliament.

For almost a year there was only desultory fighting in Yorkshire. The Fairfaxes encamped for a time on Harden Moor, near Bingley, and from this base fended off an attack on Bradford by royalists from York. In the winter of 1642, Lord Fairfax established his headquarters at Tadcaster, whilst his son Thomas guarded the crossing of the Wharfe at Wetherby.

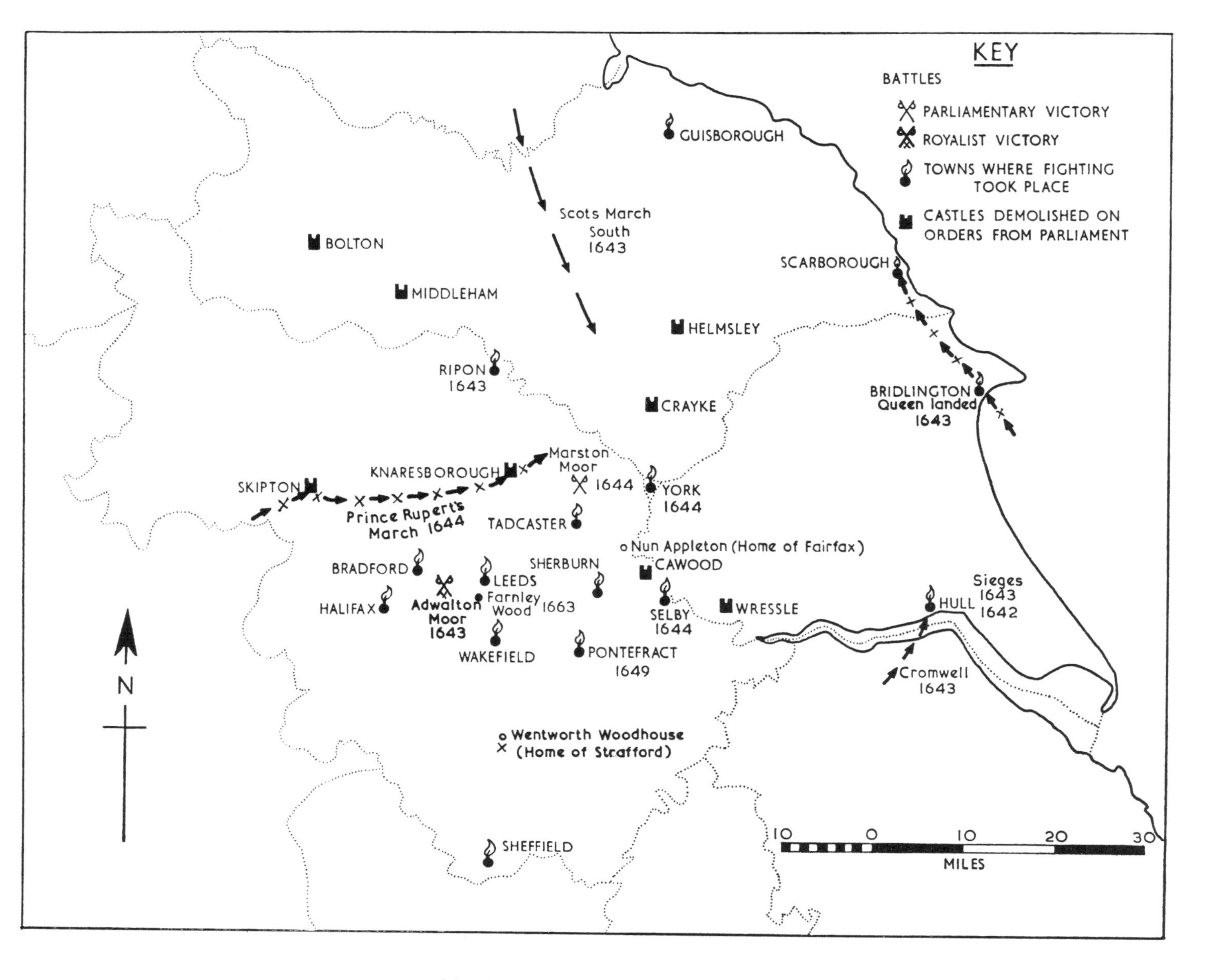

Map 8. Yorkshire in the Civil War.

Newcastle, who had taken command of the royalists in December, drove the Fairfaxes out of Tadcaster and Wetherby and advanced on Pontefract, Leeds and Wakefield. Bradford and Halifax successfully resisted. It was during this period that the tower of the parish church (now Bradford Cathedral) was protected by wool sacks from damage by the cannon shot of the attackers.

Early in 1643 the siege of Skipton Castle began. The Cliffords, who were strong supporters of the King, were surrounded by parliamentarians, including John Lambert of Carlton near Kirkby Malham, who became one of the military leaders of the parliamentary forces.

At the end of January 1643 the parliamentarians counter-attacked, re-occupied Leeds and Wakefield and forced Newcastle to withdraw to his headquarters in York. Royalist fortunes changed in February 1643, when the Queen landed at Bridlington from Holland, and, despite narrowly missing being killed in a bombardment by parliamentary ships, made her way via Boynton Hall to York. Queen Henrietta Maria, the sister of Louis XIII of France, was a woman of some spirit and charisma, and during her stay in Yorkshire she persuaded many influential figures (some of whom were waverers and some who had been thought to be strong parliamentarians) to rally to the royalist side. These included Sir Hugh Cholmley of Whitby, who brought Scarborough Castle over to the King; Sir William Strickland of Boynton; and, it is suspected, the Hothams, father and son, of Hull. The governor and his son, who had fought bravely in support of the Fairfaxes in 1642, were arrested in June 1643 on suspicion of opening negotiations with Newcastle, in order to turn the city over to the King. They were both executed as traitors to Parliament in 1645.

With the boost to his morale – and also to the *matériel* – which the Queen's presence in York provided, Newcastle felt strong enough to take the initiative against Fairfax. He moved south to Pontefract, occupied Sheffield Castle, which had been taken by parliamentary forces without a fight in 1642, and secured Hallamshire for the King. In June, the Queen rode to Oxford to join her husband, content that the situation in Yorkshire was secure. On 30 June 1643 the Fairfaxes advanced from Bradford to meet a force of 10,000 royalists on Aldwalton Moor, between Bradford and Wakefield. Outnumbered by more than two to one, they were soundly beaten, leaving 700 of their infantry dead on the battlefield and losing hundreds more as prisoners. Lord Fairfax retreated to Bradford and his son to Halifax, but by the middle of the summer the woollen towns had fallen to the royalists; Bradford was sacked and all Yorkshire except Hull was lost to Parliament.

Lord Fairfax was invited to become governor of Hull and arrived there in time to prepare for the defence of the city against the siege, which Newcastle mounted in September. Thomas was forced to abandon Bradford, and after a perilous journey along the south shore of the Humber, joined his father in Hull, and the siege was raised in October.

17. (*right*) View down the nave of Fountains Abbey, one of the finest Cistercian houses in Europe.

18. (*below*) Beningbrough Hall, North Yorkshire: the house from the south-west. Completed in 1716 on the site of a Tudor house, by William Thornton, a pupil of Nicholas Hawksmoor.

19. Merchant Adventurers Hall, Fossgate, York, dating from the 14th and 15th centuries.

20. River buses moored after dark on the river Ouse by the floodlit Guildhall, York.

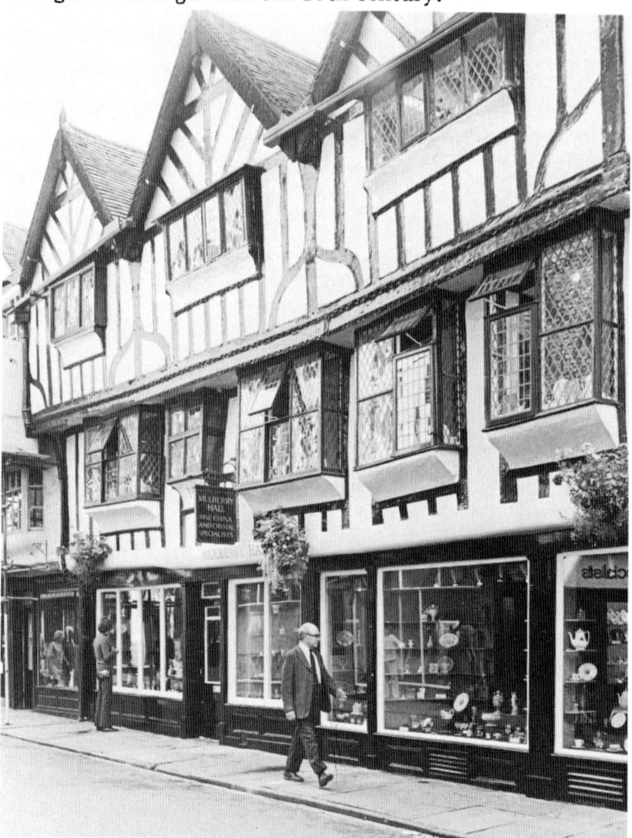

21. Stonegate, York, a well preserved street of timbered houses from the 15th to 17th centuries, and elegant Georgian buildings from the 18th century.

22. Mansion House, St Helen's Square, York, an early Georgian building, the home of the Lord Mayor and Lady Mayoress during their year of office.

23. York Minster at night. A predominantly Gothic church, dedicated to St Peter, built of magnesian limestone from Tadcaster between the 11th and 15th centuries on the foundations of a 7th-century church destroyed by fire in 1069.

24. Delves Cottage, a 17th-century thatched cottage at Egton Bridge, near Whitby.

25. Interior view of the same cruck cottage.

Parliament's turn came in the following year, when the Scots were persuaded to intervene. They were told that, if the King won, their Presbyterian Church would be in danger, while if Parliament won there was a hope that Presbyterian ideas would affect the teaching and organisation of the established Church of England. While the Scots advanced against Newcastle's forces in Northumberland and Durham, the Fairfaxes began to attack from Hull. Sir William Constable led a force which recovered the East Riding and reached as far along the coast as Whitby, although failing to take Scarborough Castle. Meanwhile Lambert recaptured Bradford and the two Fairfaxes defeated a force of 1,700 men under Sir John Belasyse, at Selby, and cleared much of the area south of York of royalists. Newcastle retreated to York, with some 8,000 men, and prepared for a siege. Meanwhile the Scots bypassed York and joined with the Fairfaxes at Tadcaster. The siege of York began on 3 June and lasted for 25 days. It was raised when the Fairfaxes heard of the imminent arrival of a large force under the command of the King's dashing nephew, Prince Rupert.

Rupert, with 6,000 foot soldiers and 7,000 cavalry, swept across the Pennines from Lancashire, proceeded down Wharfedale to Otley, and reached Knaresborough at the end of June. He out-manoeuvred the Fairfaxes, who were waiting for him near Skip Bridge on the Nidd, and, crossing into the city on a bridge of boats, led 2,000 of his cavalry into York on 1 July. The Scots and the parliamentary forces decided to withdraw to Tadcaster, but the impetuous Rupert broke out from York, crossed the river at Poppleton and attempted to intercept them. Battle was joined on Marston Moor on 2 July.

The Battle of Marston Moor involved the largest forces of troops of any battle in the Civil War. Rupert had at his disposal some 11,000 foot soldiers and 7,000 cavalry; and the parliamentary forces numbered some 27,000 men, of whom about 9,000 were cavalry. An artillery duel began at about three o'clock in the afternoon, but the real fighting did not begin until three hours later. Oliver Cromwell, who was in charge of a contingent of 2,500 horse which he had raised the previous year in the eastern counties, distinguished himself in an engagement near Tockwith, in which he was slightly wounded, although claims on his behalf to have made the decisive breakthrough are contested by Scottish historians, who give the credit to David Leslie, in command of a squadron of Scots. The issue was not decided until 10 p.m., and in fact it seemed at one point that the royalists would prevail (a message to this effect was actually sent to the royalist governor of Tickhill Castle) but again Cromwell is given the credit for rallying the parliamentary forces and striking the decisive blow. Rupert escaped and made his way to Lancashire by way of Wensleydale. Newcastle rode to Scarborough and took ship to the Continent.

Cromwell reported afterwards that 'We charged their regiments of foot with our horse and routed all we charged . . . God made them as stubble to our swords'.

Marston Moor memorial

After Marston Moor the parliamentary generals dispersed. Cromwell went first to Doncaster and then back to the eastern counties; Lambert was occupied with the siege of Pontefract Castle, which fell in 1645; and the Fairfaxes remained in York, Ferdinando as governor of the city until 1645, when he was forced to resign under the terms of the Self-Denying Ordinance. Thomas Fairfax used York as a base while subduing the remaining Yorkshire castles which still held out for the King. These included Knaresborough, which sustained a six-week siege; and Helmsley, where Thomas was badly wounded. The last Yorkshire castle to fall to the parliamentary forces was Skipton, the stronghold of the Cliffords, which was taken in December 1645. Between 1646 and 1647 Parliament ordered the destruction of eight famous Yorkshire castles, so that they should be rendered incapable of use in war; Knaresborough, Cawood, Middleham, Bolton, Crayke, Helmsley, Wressle and Skipton were all included. Thomas Fairfax was placed at the head of the New Model Army at the beginning of 1645.

The triumph of Parliament in Yorkshire was soon followed by the total rout of the King's forces by the New Model Army at Naseby, 14 June 1645, and by Charles' surrender in January 1647.

Before long, however, the unpopularity of some of the measures introduced by Parliament – and particularly, a rift between Parliament and the Army – produced a coalition of forces favourable to a royalist revival. The Scots changed sides, dissatisfied with the treatment of Presbyterians who wanted a reconciliation with the King. War broke out again in 1648. Several Yorkshire gentry changed sides and Pontefract and Scarborough castles were again in royalist hands. Cromwell and Lambert were active in Yorkshire during this second phase of the Civil War, ranging wide across the county, from Doncaster and Pontefract to Knottingley and Knaresborough. On one occasion in August 1648, Cromwell made 'a lion like spring across the Yorkshire fells', from Knaresborough, where he had arrived from Pontefract to give support to Lambert, to Preston, where the Scots were harassing the Parliamentary forces in Lancashire. The King, who had been imprisoned by order of Parliament in Carisbrooke Castle, was seized by the army; and a Parliament purged of those, like the Presbyterians, who favoured a compromise, established a court to try the King. Fifteen Yorkshiremen were among the judges and six were present at his execution on 30 January 1649. Pontefract Castle held out for another six weeks, and was the last place in England to surrender to the Roundheads. At the request of the inhabitants, the castle was demolished.

In the decade which followed Cromwell recognised some of Yorkshire's needs; for example, the rising towns of Leeds and Halifax were given representation in the Parliaments of 1654 and 1656. In general, people in Yorkshire, like those in other parts of the country, soon tired of his rule, and even some of his most prominent supporters began to favour the restoration of Charles II, which was achieved in 1660, two years after Cromwell's death. Indeed, the greatest of them all, Thomas Lord Fairfax (his father, Ferdinando, had died during the Civil War and Thomas now held the family title), led the commissioners sent by Parliament to meet the exiled King in Holland, and to make the necessary arrangements. Fairfax refused all payment for doing what he had thought right, and again retired to his house at Nun Appleton. He would have nothing to do with the Government's policy of punishing the puritans and republicans.

We hear of him again in connection with the Farnley Wood Plot of 1663, in which 200 men opposed to Charles and his government, many of them persecuted Nonconformists and old officers of Cromwell's army, met in Farnley Wood, near Leeds, to try to overcome Charles' government by force. They soon scattered and nothing came of their plotting, for the Government was forewarned. Almost the last letter Fairfax is known to have written was one to the King (who owed him so much) asking for reasonable and lenient treatment for the plotters. In fact, 21 of them were executed! The laws against Nonconformists were made more cruel than ever; one of them, the Conventicle Act of 1664, was a direct result of the plot. It was not until 1880 that people in England who preferred to worship God 'chapel' fashion were treated in every way equal to their fellow citizens who preferred to attend public worship in the parish churches. There were many reasons for the notion that 'church' went with loyalty, 'chapel' with treason. One of them, which certainly had some force 300 years ago, was the last Yorkshire 'rebellion' – the Farnley Wood Plot, the real end of the Civil War in Yorkshire.

XII The City of York

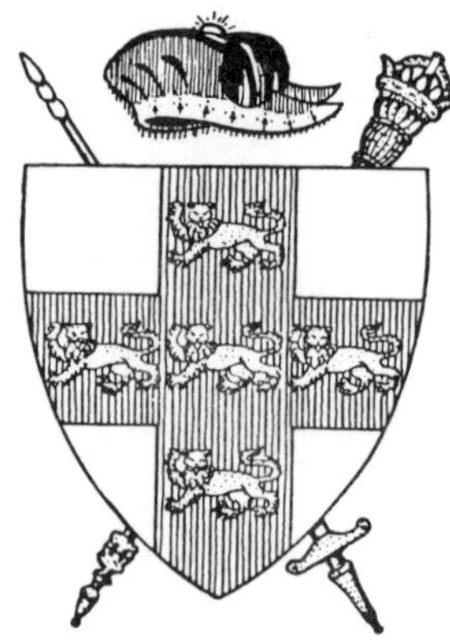
Arms of City of York

The City of York stands at a crossing-place of important routeways, and it was probably for this reason that the Romans chose it as a garrison town for their forces in northern England. The tidal river Ouse was navigable as far as York, and even beyond, as also was its tributary, the Foss, which joins the Ouse a few hundred yards to the south of the Roman city walls. The Ouse provides a water route to the Humber estuary and the North Sea and thus it was possible for York to become a major European inland port, from Roman times until the changes in European commerce which occurred at the time of the Age of Discovery in the late 15th century. The Vale of York, in the centre of which the city lies, is subjected to flooding from time to time, but the fortunate positioning of a line of glacial moraines provides a dry route from east to west across the Vale, connecting the Yorkshire Wolds with the Pennines. The east-west route crosses the Ouse valley at a point where the river is fordable – and also bridgeable.

Roman York

The first wooden fortress of Roman *Eboracum* was built in A.D. 71, under the orders of Petillius Cerialis, governor of Britain and son-in-law of the Emperor Vespasian. This wooden structure, protected by an earthen rampart, was replaced by stone buildings at the beginning of the second century and was strengthened and enlarged throughout the next 150 years. During a rebellion in A.D. 197 considerable damage was done to the walls, but this was soon repaired. Apart from this disturbance *Eboracum* had a relatively peaceful time until the barbarian invasion of the fourth century and the outpouring of Picts across Hadrian's Wall. During this time it became a great commercial centre as well as a garrison town. It was, however, the major forward outpost from which the defence of northern England against the Celtic tribes of Scotland was conducted. Early in the third century the status of a Roman *colonia* was conferred on the civil settlement which had grown up around the garrison. The Emperor Severus, who used York as his base for campaigns against invaders from Scotland between A.D. 208 and 211, raised *Eboracum* to the position of administrative capital of the province of *Britannia Inferior*. He died in the city in A.D. 211.

Relations between the Romans and the Celtic Parisii of the neighbouring areas of East Yorkshire were, however, good and York became the market centre for agricultural produce from the surrounding countryside. The last great reconstruction of the fortifications was carried out under the personal direction of the Emperor Constantius Chlorus, at the beginning of the fourth century. The ruins of one of the towers built by Constantius – the 10-sided, Multangular or West Angular Tower – and a short length of wall can be seen in the Museum gardens, adjoining the present city library. Constantius died in *Eboracum* in A.D. 306 and his son, Constantine the Great, was proclaimed Emperor there. During the fourth century the city became a centre of Romano-British Christianity.

There are many Roman remains in the museums in York which testify to the existence of a thriving city with administrative, military and commercial functions, which at its peak of prosperity was the home of some 15,000 people. These include Roman baths, underground temples to the god Mithras, Samian ware pottery, tiles stamped with the numbers of the IX and VI Legions, and craftsmen's tools. A statue of a Roman legionary in the museum in the grounds of St Mary's Abbey is considered to be one of the best examples of Romano-British art to be found in Britain.

Anglian York

The departure of the Romans from Britain at the beginning of the fifth century was followed by a period of confusion and disorder. When the Angles came to York they found a ruined city, which they occupied and made the capital of their kingdom of Deira, which later merged into Northumbria. King Edwin of Northumbria (A.D. 616-632) made York his capital, and also built the first wooden church on the site where the Minster now stands.

Danish York

In A.D. 866 a Danish force, led by Ivar and Halfdan, sons of the Viking chief Ragnar Lothbrok (Leather Breeches), sailed up the Humber and the Ouse and sacked York. They placed a puppet king, Egbert, on the throne and left for further conquests in the Midlands. Egbert and the Danes successfully resisted attempts by the Northumbrians to recapture the city, in 867 and 872, and York, known as Jorvik, soon became the capital of the Danish kingdom. The discovery in 1976 of the remains of the Viking settlement, during building operations in Coppergate, has led to the development of the Jorvik Viking Centre, where an imaginative reconstruction of the way of life of the Vikings over 1,000 years ago has been created. It was a town of many traders and craftsmen. Their wooden homes, arranged in streets, were built amid the remains of the Roman and Anglian settlements. They kept domestic animals; grew corn and vegetables; worked metal, leather and wood for tools and ornaments; and wove cloth and cured animal skins

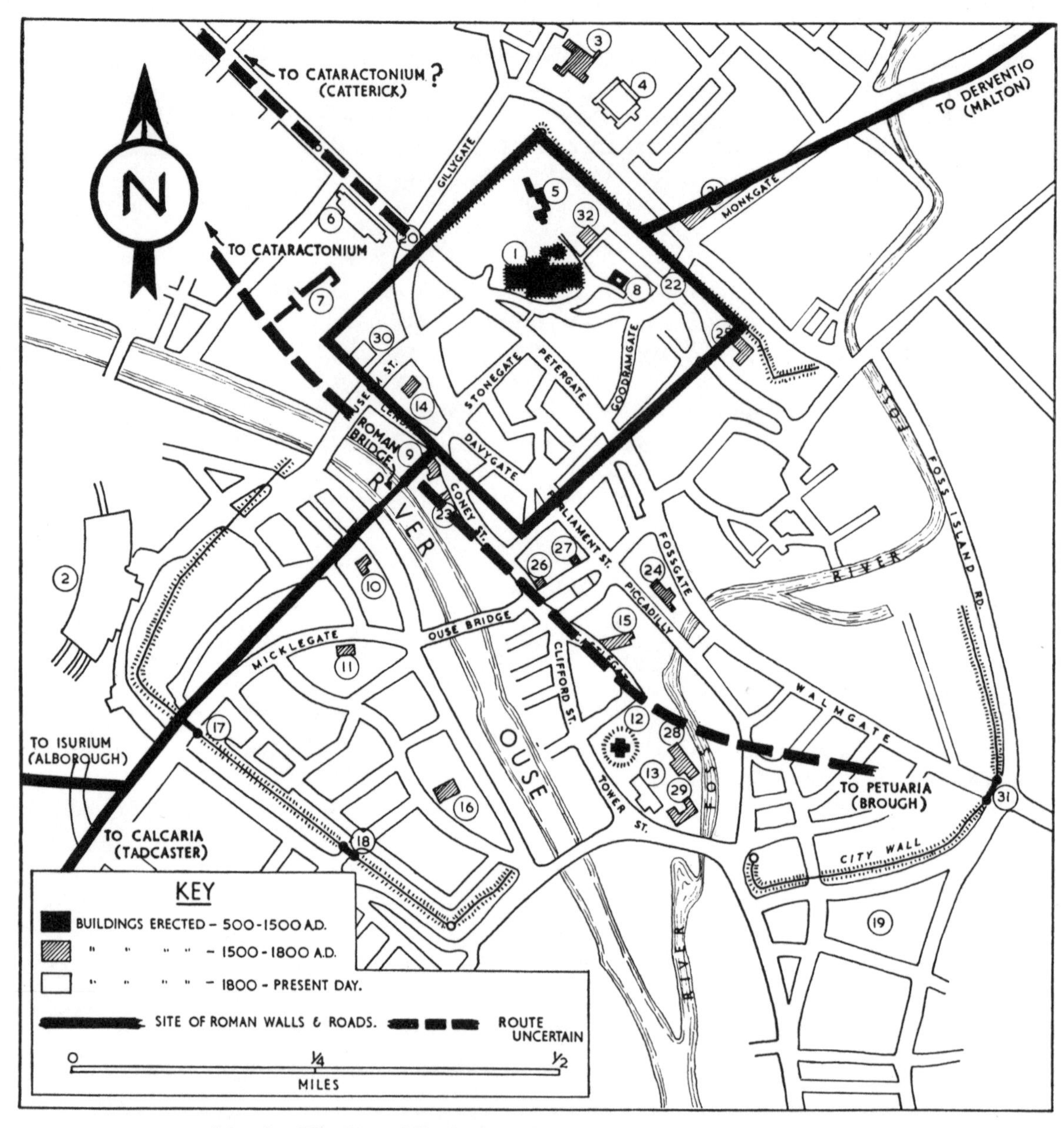

Map 9. The City of York: from Roman times to the present day.

KEY TO MAP OF YORK

1. Minster.
2. Railway Station.
3. Archbishop Holgate's Grammar School.
4. St. John's Training College.
5. Minster Library.
6. Art Gallery.
7. St. Mary's Abbey ruins.
8. St. William's College.
9. Mansion House and Guildhall.
10. All Hallows Church.
11. St. Martin-cum-Gregory.
12. Clifford's Tower.
13. Law Courts.
14. Assembly Rooms.
15. St. Mary's Church.
16. St. Mary's (Elder).
17. Micklegate Bar.
18. Victoria Bar.
19. Cattle Market.
20. Bootham Bar.
21. St. Maurice's Church.
22. Monk Bar.
23. St. Martin's Church.
24. Merchants' Hall.
25. Merchant Taylors Hall.
26. St. Michael's Church.
27. All Saints Church.
28. Castle Museum.
29. The Old Prison.
30. Public Library.
31. Walmgate Bar.

for their clothing. In the mid-10th century Eric Bloodaxe, a famous sea-rover, invaded Northumbria and took York, but in A.D. 954 he was expelled and later killed and the Viking kingdom of York came to an end. The kingdom of York was re-absorbed into Northumbria.

Bootham Bar and Minster

Norman York

Over a century later, at the time of the Norman Conquest, York had a population of over 8,000 inhabitants living within the protection of the city walls. Although there was a setback to its development because of the devastation of Yorkshire at the time of the Harrying of the North, there was a steady growth during the 12th century. The Normans enclosed a wide area of ground within a high earthen rampart, partly placed over the Roman walls, and in the 12th and 13th centuries a wall and gates were built to reinforce the defences. Within this protective barrier the medieval city grew and flourished. The stonework of Bootham and Micklegate Bars shows some of its earliest defences.

The Minster

When the Normans came to York there had already been at least two, perhaps three, churches on the site of the Minster. The first Norman Archbishop, Thomas of Bayeux, built anew on the foundations of the last Saxon church, but, 50 years after his death, his successor built yet again, as Thomas's church was thought to be too small. Hardly had a generation passed before plans were being put into effect to build yet one more church, larger and more majestic than any of the others had been. It is this church, the fifth or sixth on the site, which is seen today. Archbishop Walter de Gray began the work by demolishing the remaining transept of Thomas of Bayeux's church, and replacing it with the present magnificent south transept in 1241. By the time of his death in 1255, the north transept and probably the Five Sisters window were already finished. The next great period of building activity was at the end of the 13th and in the first half of the 14th century, when the Norman nave was replaced, and a chapter house added. In the late 14th century the Norman choir was replaced, and the finishing of this work, about 1400, completed the interior structure.

Medieval York

During the Middle Ages the city grew, and by 1377 it had a population of over 13,000. As there was less danger of civil war and invasion, there was less need to live behind the protection of defensive walls. So in York, as in other walled towns, gradually the houses began to spread to the districts outside the walls. Throughout much of the Middle Ages, however, the citizens of York felt safe only when they were huddled together within the security of the ramparts. This explains the narrowness of the streets like Stonegate and the Shambles, which were within the

York Minster gargoyle

Gatehouse of Minster Close

walls. The overcrowding gave rise to problems of health and sanitation. There was no main sewer, and household refuse was thrown into open drains, which carried it into the Ouse and the Foss.

The incidence of plague was as common in York as in other cities, and it continued into the 16th and 17th centuries. There were outbreaks in 1538, 1551 and 1631. The last of these raged in the suburbs, but the inner city was spared its worst effects by the vigilance of the gatekeepers, who denied entry to any they suspected might have been in contact with the infection. However, medieval York was not only a city of smells and squalor; it contained many beautiful buildings. Amongst the best of those now standing is the King's Manor (now part of the University of York). This was originally the house of the Abbot of St Mary's. After the Reformation it was used as the official home of the Lord President of the Council of the North. Much of it was rebuilt by the great Earl of Strafford. One may still see over a doorway the griffin supporters of his coat of arms. The fact that he had placed his private coat of arms on the King's property was remembered against him, with other serious charges, when he was accused of treason, condemned and executed in 1641.

The moats which defended the medieval city have long since disappeared, although there is an interesting portion of them remaining in Lord Mayor's Walk. The ancient ramparts and the city walls which stand on them are there to this day, with their five great gatehouses, or bars, and one remaining postern gate, that of Fishergate. It is possible to walk on the top of the walls a great part of the way round the city.

Georgian York

Some of the most interesting and attractive buildings in York today are those which were built during the 18th century, when the city was a centre of fashion and style, almost as famous as Bath. The 'trend setters' of the time took refuge from the London season in York and, later, Harrogate. The racecourse on the Knavesmire and the Assembly Rooms, built in 1736, were the focal points round which the social life of Georgian York revolved. The Mansion House, opened in 1726, was unique amongst the civic buildings of the kingdom, as it served as the residence of the Lord Mayor and his wife during their term of office. The title of Lord Mayor dates from 1389, only London having established the office earlier. There is one odd respect in which York claims a privilege which London does not have. The Lord Mayor is entitled to be addressed as 'My Lord' only for his term of office, but his wife can insist on being called 'My Lady' for the rest of her life.

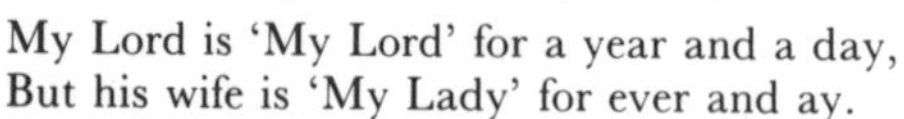

My Lord is 'My Lord' for a year and a day,
But his wife is 'My Lady' for ever and ay.

Cigar Store Indian

The Guildhall, which stands adjacent to the Mansion House, was originally built in the 15th century, but it was badly damaged during an air raid in 1942. The present structure is a reconstruction, incorporating surviving remnants of the old building, which was opened by Queen Elizabeth, the Queen Mother, in 1960. Amongst its treasures is a stained glass window with five lights, which depict aspects of the history of York, from Norman times to the bombing raid of 1942.

From 1396 until 1974 York had an unusual position in local government. Lying at the meeting point of the three Ridings, it was not within any of them and was a county with its own Sheriff. From the time of Henry VI until the 19th century it had some jurisdiction over the Ainsty (see map below). York is now a district within the county of North Yorkshire.

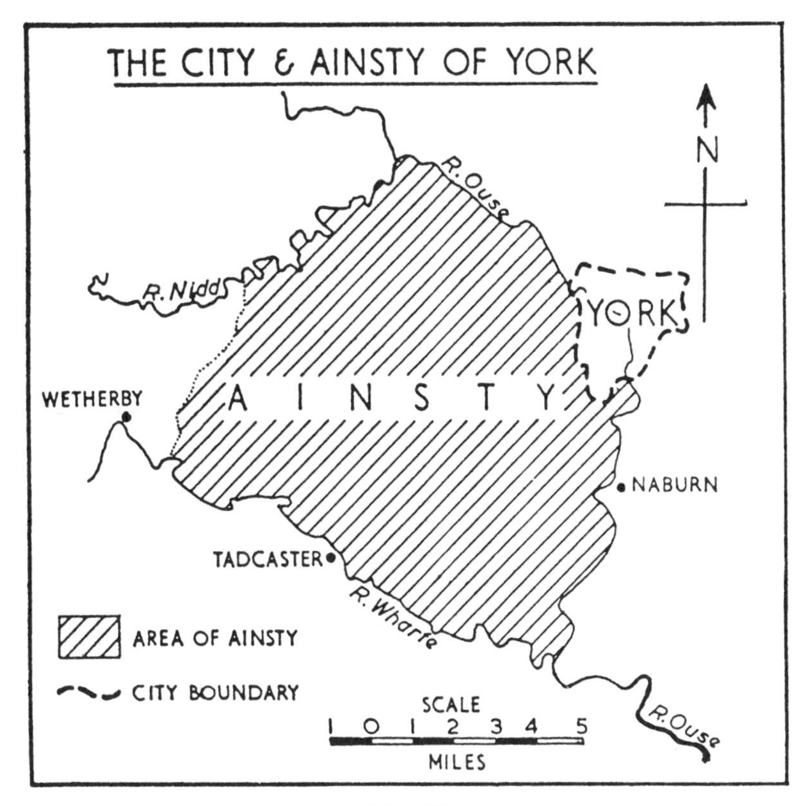

Map 10.

The Industrial Revolution

The impact of the Industrial Revolution was felt in York mainly through the efforts of George Hudson, 'The Railway King', who told George Stephenson, the railway engineer, that it was his ambition to 'mak all t'railways cum to York.' He made York into a major railway centre, with locomotive works, repair shops and associated crafts. Being situated away from the coalfields, York's industries – painting, glassware, furniture making and above all chocolates, with which the names of Rowntree and Terry are associated – were not of a kind which caused pollution.

Arms of the See of York

Religious life in York

York is, of course, of great importance in being the centre of government of the Northern Province of the Church of England. Its Archbishop ranks next to the Archbishop of Canterbury in religious matters, and is only two steps below him in precedence in secular affairs. York is also of great importance in the life of religious bodies other than the Church of England. The Roman Catholics have always been strong there, and in Bar Convent they have the oldest Roman Catholic school in England continuously existing on the same site. Its treasures include relics of Catholics who suffered martyrdom for their faith, as for example the mummified hand of St Margaret Clitherow, the butcher's wife who was crushed to death in 1686 and who was canonised in 1970. There are also mementoes of Thomas Thwing, the last of the English martyr priests, who was hanged, drawn and quartered in 1680. For centuries the religious, civil and industrial life of York has been enriched by the presence of a very active and influential group of members of the Society of Friends (the Quakers). To them York owes not only great industries but also very valuable educational and philanthropic institutions, schools and hospitals.

Modern York

The rich architectural heritage which has been preserved in York has given the city a high place in the list of tourist attractions for visitors to Britain, and York has been quick to take advantage of the opportunities afforded by the country's fastest growing industry. An increasing proportion of its citizens are now engaged in catering and in commercial, educational and entertainment activities directed to the needs of visitors.

In October 1963 the first group of 216 students were enrolled at the new University, established on a site at Heslington Hall, on the outskirts of the city. It is surprising that York did not have a university before this time, as it has always been a seat of learning, with the centuries old Minster Library; a grammar school tradition stretching back to the seventh century; St John's College; the Art and Technical Colleges founded in the first half of the 19th century; and a rich variety of religious schools, from the Bar Convent, established in 1686 to the Quaker foundations of Bootham (1822) and the Mount School (1831). The Quakers also founded the York Settlement in 1909, which has been the mainstay of the vigorous adult education life of York. A petition to found a university was launched in 1652, but it failed to raise any interest in Parliament and sank without trace. Today, with a flourishing university, the educational and cultural life of the city is as rich and full of vitality as it has ever been throughout its long history.

York Devil

XIII Agriculture in Yorkshire

Farm cart

Yorkshire was predominantly an agricultural county until well into the 19th century, and even in 1851 more Yorkshire people, especially men, 'were employed about horses than on the railways, and there were more handicraft blacksmiths than men in great iron works'.

Farming has always been an important occupation and the land in Yorkshire has been farmed since Neolithic times. At first agriculture was a necessary pursuit for almost all the population, and subsistence farming was the rule. Specialisation and the growth of trade in agricultural produce began even before the Norman Conquest, but it became firmly established as a result of the activities of the Cistercian monks in the 12th century. As many of the Cistercian houses were established in upland areas, sheep farming played an important part in their economy. Monks from other orders also became involved in sheep rearing on an extensive scale. At its peak, Fountains Abbey used thousands of acres of land in Craven, and owned over 15,000 sheep. Bolton Priory grazed its sheep in Wharfedale and Malhamdale; Sawley Abbey's lands extended from the Trough of Bowland to Gargrave; and Kirkstall had pasture in Bessacarr for 1,000 sheep and 40 mares. The monasteries were involved in other forms of agriculture – Jervaulx in Wensleydale kept large herds of cattle and was also involved in industry, but their greatest contribution to the economy of the realm was derived from their sheep and from the export trade in wool.

Yorkshire wool was exported throughout Europe, especially to Italy and northern Europe. It is symbolic that the Lord Chancellor still sits on the Woolsack when he presides over the meetings of the House of Lords, a custom which goes back to monastic times when wool was one of the mainstays of the English economy. The drovers' roads which were used by the monks can still be traced as green tracks across the Pennines and North Yorkshire moors. Later drovers (the Scottish cattlemen) used them, although they also made use of newer routes when they brought their cattle to market in Yorkshire.

Taking cloth to market

Traditional farming was based on the open-field system, by which a local economy was largely dependent on three large arable fields and a common pasture surounding the village. This was a very inefficient method of farming since usually only two of the arable fields were cultivated each year, with the third lying fallow to allow for the natural restoration of the soil. A three course rotation, of rye or wheat, oats or barley and then fallow, ensured that each field would be used differently each year. In some areas, particularly around Harrogate, the fallow would be every second or third year, with the result that it took longer for the field to recover. A field was kept fallow because of ignorance about methods of manuring the soil. At the same time the selective breeding of animals was severely restricted by the practice of allowing free grazing on the common land, where different breeds intermixed and disease was difficult to control. Farming improvements were difficult to achieve because of the need for common agreement among the tenants who held scattered strips of land in the fields. The open-field system brought many social benefits to communal village life but these were outweighed by methods which were becoming increasingly uneconomic. Only by joining strips of land together and enclosing the larger fields with walls and hedges could improvement take place.

Enclosure had in fact been carried out in a piecemeal fashion for hundreds of years. The decline of the feudal system began long before the Black Death of the 14th century, but the depopulation of the peasantry at that time greatly accelerated the process. Enclosure of open-fields, especially near lowland villages, began on a large scale in Tudor times. Common lands were also enclosed to provide sheep runs, as is evident from the protest of Sir Thomas More in 1517, who wrote of the 'unsatiable cormarauntes' who 'compasse about and inclose many thousand akers of ground'. Great tracts of land in the Vale of Mowbray and in Cleveland had been enclosed well before the enclosure movement of the 18th and early 19th centuries, by which time open-field and enclosure already existed side by side in the East Riding. In Ripon and Harrogate enclosure occurred in the 17th century through the consolidation of various strips of land by purchase and exchange and sometimes the renting of adjacent strips to create a large field. At Knaresborough and Scriven such enclosure was often affected by the right of average, whereby any occupant of the common arable fields could graze cattle over all the land after the harvesting of the cornfields.

Although the expanding industrial areas of the West Riding and elsewhere and the proximity of canal and river transport influenced local agricultural specialisation, the major determining factors were geology and climate. By the late 18th century the marginal lands of the North York Moors and Upper Pennines still supported sheep and little else while the highly cultivated areas of Holderness in the East Riding, where the majority of people were employed in agriculture, produced wheat, barley and oats and exported surplus corn from Hull to London and Europe. The North Riding was famous for horse breeding, including hunters and chargers. In the Vale of York and Vale of Mowbray, cattle were grazed and then moved by drovers southwards and many farmers in the Pennines depended for their livelihood on the rearing of young stock to be fattened on farms in the midlands and the south of the country. Some of the old drovers' routes are still marked by the names

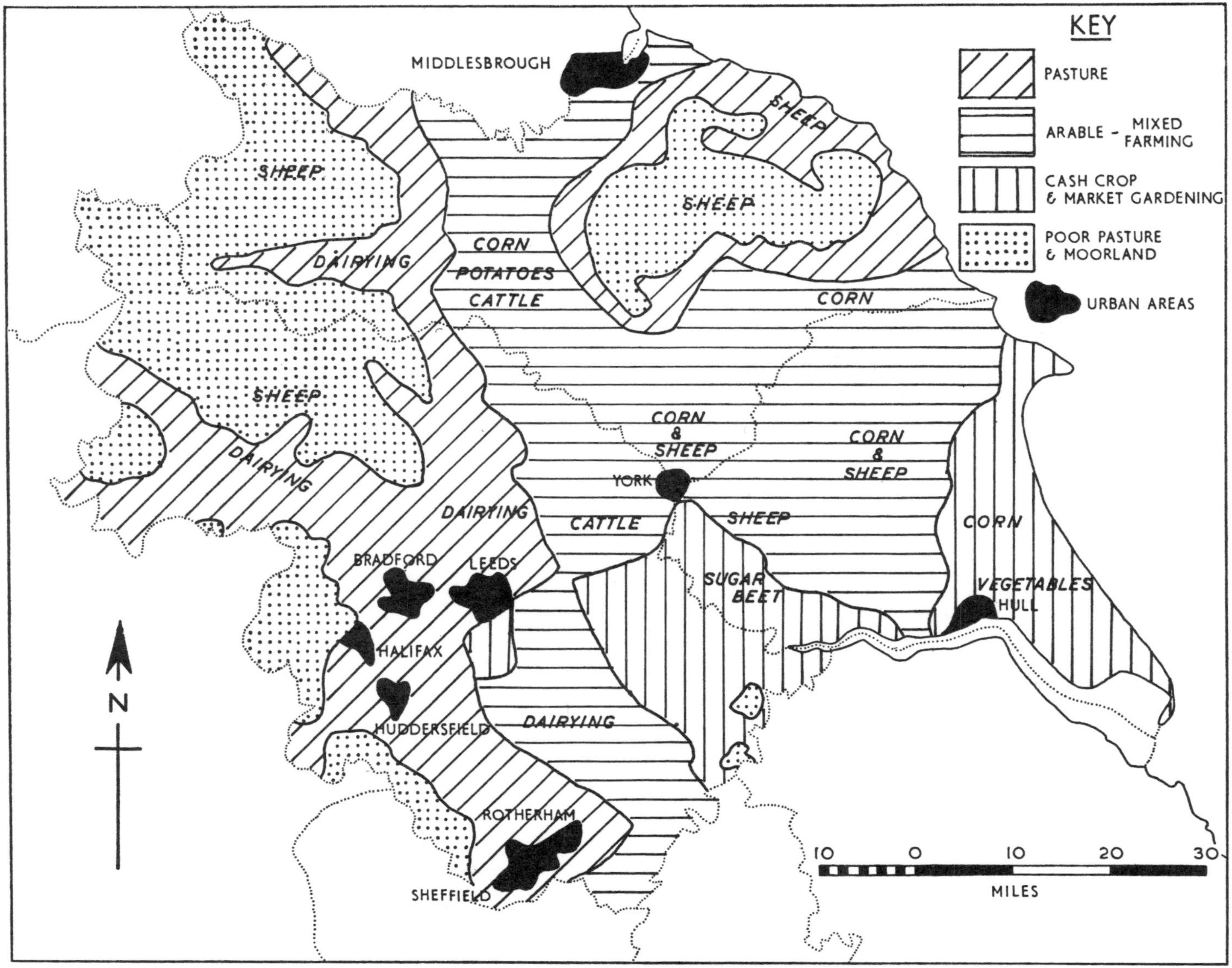

Map 11. Yorkshire Agriculture.

of inns, such as the *Drovers Inn* at Boroughbridge. There was a mixture of arable and pasture farming throughout much of the West Riding and although some produce was sent to East Lancashire or London, including butter and bacon from Nidderdale, most of the wool, milk, butter, cheese and bacon was sent to local manufacturing towns where demand increased as the populations grew.

An account of the increasing interaction between industry and agriculture can be found in the Board of Agriculture County Reports, compiled by William Marshall, perhaps the most reliable of the late 18th and early 19th century travel writers. In the West Riding it was reported that 'the greatest part of the ground is there occupied by persons who do not consider farming as a business, but regard it only as a matter of convenience. The manufacturer has his enclosure, wherein he keeps milch cows for supporting his family and horses for carrying his goods to market and bringing back raw materials. This will apply to the most part of the land adjoining to the manufacturing towns.'

The greater demands for farm produce created by the rising populations of the manufacturing districts could not be met by local agriculture alone, and production of foodstuffs throughout the county had to increase. Only by enclosing more land could this be achieved. Enclosure often involved the use of a private Act of Parliament, for which a local landowner could petition if he was supported by the owners of three-quarters of the value of the land. This meant that a single large landowner could overcome the opposition of many smaller landowners. In fact, the whole process of enclosure was weighted in favour of the landowner. Many people who were directly affected, such as those who rented cottages with rights of access to the common land, or squatters, had no automatic right to be consulted. Only those who could afford the time and the cost would be able to travel from Yorkshire to London to register a complaint.

In 1793 the Duke of Leeds obtained an Act of Parliament to enclose his land at Wakefield. Written into the Act was a clause whereby no one could interfere with the Duke's right to work mines and get minerals. Anyone adversely affected by mining would be compensated, not by the Duke, but by all the allottees of the commons and waste grounds, which would include those whose property might be damaged. Those who held allotments on certain parts of the land were affected by a special clause: 'They are forbidden to put up any House, Building or Erection of any kind on one part for 20, on another for 40, on another for 60, years unless the Duke consents', the object being 'thereby the more advantageously to enable the said Duke, his Heirs and Assigns, to work his colliery in and upon the same Moor'.

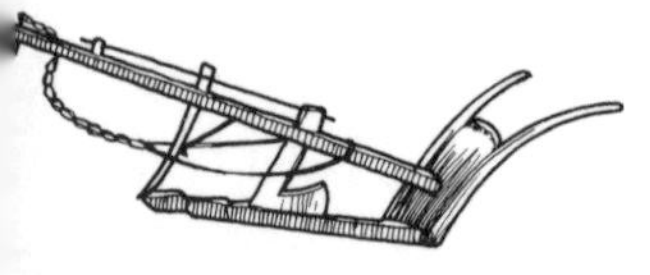
Eighteenth-century plough

The effects of enclosure were far-reaching. Many of the improvements in agriculture took place in Yorkshire, where great landowners had enough capital to exploit the opportunities for manuring, better crops, selective breeding and new farm implements. One of the improving landlords was the Marquis of Rockingham, who was Prime Minister for a brief period in 1782 and who farmed at Wentworth Woodhouse. Improvements there were such that Arthur Young, who compiled detailed first-hand accounts of agricultural conditions, commented, 'I never saw the advantages of a great fortune applied more nobly to the improvements of a country . . . Draining, the general management of grasslands and manures, among other numerous articles are, at Wentworth, carried to the utmost perfection'. One of the implements in use was the Rockingham Drill Plough, similar to the seed drill invented by Jethro Tull in 1701. Another type of seed drill was invented by Dr Hunter of York in 1790, and before the end of the century horse-drawn threshing machines were being used in the East Riding.

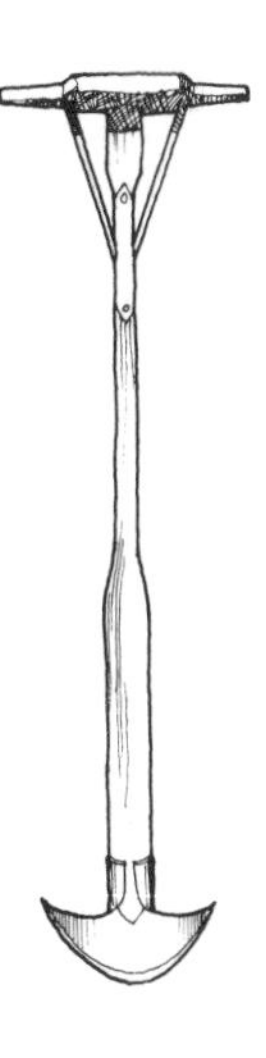

Sod spade

A more famous improver was Sir Christopher Sykes, of Sledmore, whose son, Sir Tatton Sykes, carried on in his father's footsteps. Sir Tatton erected an inscription in Sledmore village which praised his father who ' by assiduity and perseverance in building and planting and enclosing the Yorkshire Wolds in the short space of 30 years, set such an example to other owners of land, as has caused what was once a bleak and barren tract of country to become now one of the most productive and best cultivated districts of the county of York'. Miles Smith used a method of stone and turf to drain his land near Driffield around 1790. Twenty years later flat tiles were found to be more efficient in draining land in Holderness. There were also improvements in the selective breeding of animals and some farmers began to specialise in livestock breeding. The East Riding became known for its prize Leicester sheep and Short-horn cattle. Rather than adopting scientific breeding methods many farmers improved their herds by a commonsense approach of weeding out the poorer beasts and feeding the better ones well, a method which was not possible when all animals were herded together on a common land under the open-field system.

As more interest was shown in improving farming methods agricultural clubs and societies were formed to encourage better practice. At Malton and at Driffield, where a Mr. Coates bred a short-horn bull which raised a price of 500 guineas, annual prizes were awarded to the best improvements in stock breeding. In many villages cow clubs encouraged poorer farmers to build up their stock of dairy cows by insuring the animals against an early death.

Methods of improving the quality of the soil varied throughout the county. The Board of Agriculture survey of 1793 reported that up to 20 miles around Sheffield, where the effects of waste bone from the cutlers' workshops may have been observed, 'Bones of all kinds are gathered with the greatest industry and even imported from distant places. They are broke through a mill made for that purpose and sometimes laid on the ground without any mixture'. Rough pasture in the Dales was improved, creating 'intakes' by the use of local limestone. Many farmers erected kilns on outcrops of limestone on their land and coal from the

Skidby windmill

Turton cottages doorway

local thin coal measures was used for firing. Remains of small limekilns can still be seen in the Yorkshire Dales. Around the River Humber and its tidal tributaries 'warping' was used to improve the land. By means of channels and banks built by the farmer the tidal flow, especially the spring tides, deposited a salty mud sediment on the soil. Warping resulted in a very rich soil which was used as pasture and arable, with oats, beans and wheat being considered the best crops.

Although some small farm owners may have suffered as a result of the enclosure movement, the main impact was on squatters and small tenant farmers. Some became casual labourers, working on the hedging and drainage of land. Most agricultural labourers and farm servants were hired for up to a year at a time at hiring fairs or 'sittings'. In the 18th century many men and women travelled from the North and West Ridings to Malton, where they were hired for a month or more by farmers from the Wolds and Holderness. The annual Martinmas hiring fairs in the East Riding continued to attract thousands of farm servants throughout the 19th century and the practice of hiring and paying farm workers by the year continued into the 1900s.

The wages of farm workers were generally higher in the north than other parts of the country and, with the exception of haymaking and harvesting, the employment of children was not common. Many labourers were able to grow much of their own food on their own allotments and, as we have seen, many smallholders in the West Riding combined farming with weaving. The manufacturing districts of the West Riding, where there was plenty of work, began to attract farm workers from the surrounding countryside. At the same time the local production of cloth in the more remote dales areas was destroyed by the rapid growth of the urban woollen industry. Lead mining and quarrying also declined and often the only alternative to migrating to Bradford or Leeds and other manufacturing towns was to rely solely on agriculture and associated crafts.

Early nineteenth-century cradle

The numbers employed in agriculture steadily declined during the century after 1851, and since the Second World War the numbers have fallen even more rapidly, and now account for under two per cent of the work force. Nevertheless the area of the county devoted to farming has risen compared with the inter-war period; and the volume and value of agricultural production has increased dramatically. Modern agricultural techniques have made it possible for a smaller number of people to produce more from the land. Although the influence of E.E.C. agricultural policies and fluctuations in market forces have brought in new crops – as, for example, oil seed rape and other fodder crops – the broad geographical distribution of different types of arable farming and animal husbandry has not changed greatly during the last 30 years. This is because the basic factors influencing the types of agriculture practised – soils, climate, slopes, elevation – have remained the same.

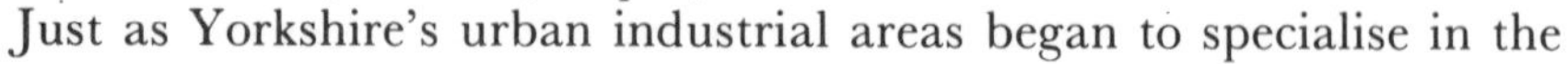

Just as Yorkshire's urban industrial areas began to specialise in the

26. 'Shandy Hall', Coxwold, once home of Laurence Sterne, author of *Tristram Shandy*, and vicar of Coxwold in the 1760s.

27. The Corn Mill, Stamford Bridge: a brick-built water mill erected in 1723 on the site of a Domesday corn mill.

28. (*left*) Holmfirth: early 19th-century mill-workers' houses.

29. (*below*) Taking a sample for testing at George Oxley and Sons' Vulcan Foundry, Sheffield.

30. (*above*) Titus Salt's 'model' factory at Saltaire, built in 1853. The model village which was built to house Salt's workers exemplified Victorian philanthropy and paternalism.

31. (*below*) Piece Hall, Halifax, opened as a cloth market in 1775, and now a centre for craft workshops, small shops and historical exhibits.

32. (*above*) Whitby Abbey, founded by St Hilda in A.D. 657. The original buildings were destroyed by the Danes in A.D. 867 and the present buildings date from the 13th century.

33. (*below*) The Humber Bridge. Officially opened by H.M. the Queen in July 1981, it is the longest single span suspension bridge in the world.

production of different manufactured goods, so the rural areas developed their own particular agricultural produce. Farming in Yorkshire still reflects this specialisation, which has been determined by type of soil, climate and marketing opportunities. Sheep graze on the higher limestone pastures, moors and rough fells of the Yorkshire Dales, still one of the most important sheep breeding areas in the country. The hardy Swaledale and Dalesbred breeds are most common and the Swaledale ram, known as a 'tup', is the symbol of the Yorkshire Dales National Park. Cattle are reared on the lower dales, where about 20 million gallons of milk and over 15 million lbs. of beef are produced annually.

Mixed arable farming is found in the lowland areas of the Vales of York and Pickering and also in the Holderness area of the East Riding. Cereal crops of corn, barley and wheat and also vegetables for local markets dominate these areas though cattle for beef and dairy products are also reared. Market gardening is important in most areas, particularly in the East Riding, providing the large conurbations with daily supplies of vegetables, lettuces and tomatoes, and also flowers.

The rural population of Yorkshire has steadily declined as people have migrated to towns and cities further afield. However there are still numbers of small farmers to be found and they, like other inhabitants of the rural areas of Yorkshire, particularly the Yorkshire Dales, are rather more concerned about the effects of improved leisure facilities and the increase of tourists than their forebears were.

Detail from the Waggoners Memorial, Sledmere, erected to honour local farm workers enlisted in World War One

XIV The Industrial Revolution in Yorkshire

Weaver's cottage doorway

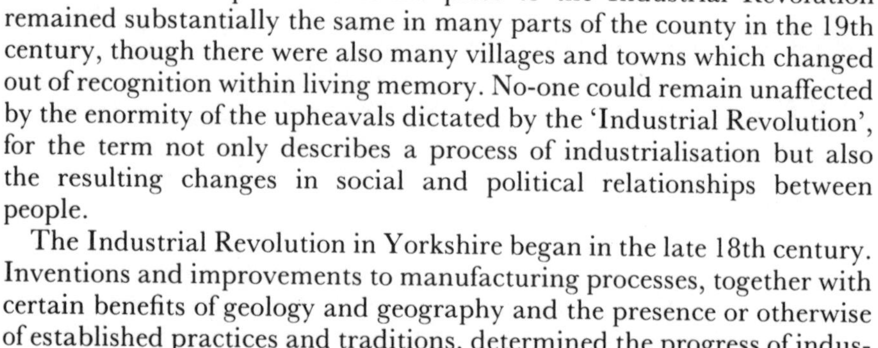

The rural landscape of Yorkshire prior to the Industrial Revolution remained substantially the same in many parts of the county in the 19th century, though there were also many villages and towns which changed out of recognition within living memory. No-one could remain unaffected by the enormity of the upheavals dictated by the 'Industrial Revolution', for the term not only describes a process of industrialisation but also the resulting changes in social and political relationships between people.

The Industrial Revolution in Yorkshire began in the late 18th century. Inventions and improvements to manufacturing processes, together with certain benefits of geology and geography and the presence or otherwise of established practices and traditions, determined the progress of industrial change. One of the major natural resources in the county is coal, and the large coal measures, covering over 3,000 square miles, stretching from the middle of the Aire Valley, southwards through Sheffield and into Derbyshire and Nottinghamshire, were important in establishing the West Riding of Yorkshire as one of the main industrial areas in the country. The coal pit remained only of local importance until the discovery of new ways of retrieving coal and using it in manufacturing processes, particularly the smelting of iron ore, although the coastal coalfields of Northumberland and Durham supplied 'sea coal' by ship to London as early as the 14th century. Steam-driven pumping engines, the first recorded in Yorkshire being a Newcomen engine at Austhorpe colliery in Leeds in 1714, enabled deeper pits to be sunk and the concealed coalfields to the East of the Pennines became accessible.

Improved steam engines, with separate condensers and applied to rotary action, were built by James Watt and Matthew Boulton, and by 1785 four of the Boulton and Watt engines were to be found in Yorkshire. Over the next 10 years 12 more engines, with a total capacity of 247 H.P., were installed, powering cotton, woollen and flax mills.

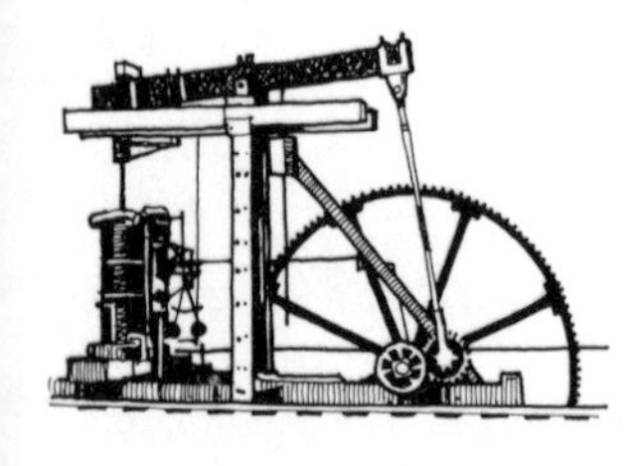

Boulton and Watt steam engine installed in Benjamin Gott's Mill, Leeds

The steam engine revolutionised the woollen textile industry of Yorkshire, which in the 13th and 14th centuries was spread thinly throughout the county. In the late Middle Ages the woollen industries in the West Riding grew rapidly. Loose manorial control allowed people to buy and sell land more easily than elsewhere, leading to smaller and smaller individual holdings and the need for a supplementary income, while the absence of guilds in the West Riding enabled easier entry into the trade compared with the declining urban centres of Beverley, Northallerton, Richmond and Ripon. The cheapness of tools and of one's own labour, plus the fact that the staple product, a coarse, narrow cloth called Kersey, could be easily woven in time for the weekly cloth markets, were additional factors in the expansion of the trade in areas like the Calder and Aire Valleys, where Halifax and Bradford were soon established as the dominant markets for the trade.

Water wheel

The iron industry in Yorkshire was revolutionised not only by the steam engine, which replaced water power to operate the bellows pumping air into the furnaces, but also by the use of coke instead of charcoal to smelt the iron ore into pig iron, a method first developed by Abraham Darby at Coalbrookdale in Shropshire, and by the improvements to the steel-making process made by Joseph Huntsman, who moved from Sheffield to Doncaster in 1740. Before these developments the old forges and workshops were located near rivers and streams, such as the tributary valleys of the Don, where waterwheels could be driven; now they began to be located within easy access to the iron ore and coal suitable for coking.

In the middle of the 19th century Henry Bessemer invented a new furnace in which air blasted out the impurities from molten pig iron. The Bessemer process was only suitable for European pig iron, which was already imported into Sheffield and where the high grade steel industry was founded. The small craft workshops, mainly producing cutlery, still continued, but now the emphasis was very much on the heavy steel industry dominated by giant firms such as John Brown and Thomas Firth, though even here steam engines often only provided motive power. At John Brown's in the 1860s armour plate, weighing an average of 31 tons, would be dragged to the rollers by some 40 men.

The changes in working conditions and the impact of new inventions on traditional forms of employment led to opposition from traditional craft workers. In the West Riding the work of skilled croppers, or shearmen, was replaced by the shearing frame and the gig mill, which could produce the same output from one-eighth of the labour employed using the traditional methods of working the cloth. Machine breakers, or 'Luddites', attempted to halt the introduction of gig mills in Leeds in 1791, though their struggle was shortlived. By 1817 there were 72 gig mills in Yorkshire and a third of the shearmen were unemployed.

Power looms began to replace the work of the handloom weavers. In Bingley, near Bradford, when an attempt was made to bring in new machinery, workers responded by trying to break it up. Luddite riots spread from Nottinghamshire into Yorkshire in 1812, when mills in Huddersfield, Leeds and Wakefield were attacked. The most serious incident was the murder of William Horsfall, of Ottiwells, near Huddersfield, who had boasted of his hatred of Luddites. Horsfall loaded a cannon and armed his men to fend off an attack on his mill. The leaders of the assault were tried at York Special Commission in January 1813.

Domestic weaver

Paddle steamer

Seventeen men were hanged, one transported for life and six were transported for seven years for administering illegal oaths.

When steam-driven power looms were introduced in the 1820s, the livelihood of handloom weavers was even more severely affected. In 1826 the Riot Act was read in Bradford when 250 protesters marched on a worsted mill. Two of the attackers were killed and several injured when shots were fired. However such demonstrations, like those against the gig mill, could at best bring only a temporary halt to the introduction of new machinery. Nine years after the riots at the Bradford worsted mill, the company had 378 power looms in operation, at which time there were over 4,000 power looms in use in textile mills throughout Yorkshire.

The specialisation and location of the basic industries of textiles, coal and iron resulted in astonishing growths of population, exemplified by Middlesbrough, which grew from a village of 25 people in 1801 to an industrial town of 75,532 by 1891. Between 1760 and 1881 the population of Leeds grew from 15,000 to 30,9119; that of Bradford grew from 8,800 to 183,032, Sheffield from 25,000 to 284,410. In the same period the population of Hull increased from 15,000 to 161,519.

As the basic industries of Yorkshire developed, so did communications and international trade. Sea ports such as Hull, which imported wool from Australia, pit props from the Baltic and Swedish iron ore, and exported finished cloth and other manufactured goods to the Continent, felt the impact of industrial change, though without the same level of human misery experienced in many of the manufacturing areas.

The rapid growth of industrial Yorkshire resulted in social conditions which shocked many people and led to government enquiries and acts of parliament. The young German poet, George Weerth, on arriving in Bradford in the 1840s, compared his journey with a descent into Hell. Here is a description of Bradford written by Frederick Engels in 1844:

> . . . Within reigns the same filth and discomfort as Leeds. The older portions of the town are built upon steep hillsides, and are narrow and irregular. In the lanes alleys and courts lie filth and debris in heaps; the houses are ruinous, dirty and miserable . . . In general, the portions of the valley bottom in which working-men's cottages have crowded between the tall factories, are amongst the worst-built and dirtiest districts of the whole town. In the newer portions of this, as of every other factory town, the cottages are more regular, being built in rows, but they share here, too, all the evils incident to the customary method of providing working-men's dwellings . . . the same is true of the remaining towns of the West Riding, especially of Barnsley, Halifax and Huddersfield.

Outbreaks of cholera occurred in Leeds and Bradford at intervals in the 19th century. In Bradford conditions generally were such that over 50 per cent of all deaths were of children under five years of age and tuberculosis alone was responsible for one death in every six of the population. Public interest was roused by Edwin Chadwick's Sanitary Report of 1842 which included reports on conditions in West Yorkshire and which laid the foundations for the passing of the Public Health Act of 1848. Under the Act Public Health Authorities were established, though progress was often slow and it took many years for conditions to improve.

It was the social conditions of the urban areas and also the working conditions in factories and mills which played a large part in the development of working class movements in Yorkshire. The Repeal of the Combination Acts in 1824 and 1825 led to the organisation of many trade unions, though most remained local organisations which were easily defeated by the masters. Legal action was taken against trade union leaders and members were blacklisted by other employers. The woolcombers in Bradford quickly tried to take advantage of the new legislation and formed the Combers and Weavers Union in 1825 to protect wages and conditions in the large mills. The woolcombers, totalling 20,000, came out on strike. The strike ended in defeat after six months, however, largely due to a lock-out declared by the masters.

These early attempts at organisation in Yorkshire were overtaken by Robert Owen's 'Grand National Consolidated Trades Union', which drew support from all areas of the country between 1832 and 1834. The Yorkshire Trades Union, which included many of the defeated Bradford woolcombers and weavers, existed alongside Owen's larger organisation, though it still adhered to the practice of secret oaths, for which the Tolpuddle Martyrs had been transported. At a meeting held on Hunslet Moor in 1834 to protest against the sentencing of the Tolpuddle men, one speaker said, 'I have known men of the strictest moral character, in the humbler walks of life, who have taken the same oath . . . to select them and transport them would almost depopulate the West Riding'. The penalties for administering illegal oaths were, as we have seen, very severe.

One method used by the masters against trade unionists was 'the Bond', which workers had to sign, agreeing not to join a trade union before they were employed. A series of strikes broke out in 1834 in protest against the practice. Three thousand workers went on strike in Leeds, and at a meeting of 10,000 workers on Hunslet Moor a request for a reasonable settlement by the employers was made. The employers refused and the protest was defeated.

The working conditions in the new steam-powered mills, in which child labour was exploited more than it had ever been in domestic manufacture, became a major issue in the 1830s. The official reports on the employment of children in factories, which recorded the comments of the victims of the factory system, are adequate testimony. A 15-year-old boy working in a Bradford worsted mill said: 'I began to work before I was five years of age. It was a worsted mill. We used to begin at six in the morning and go on till eight o'clock, sometimes nine. My legs are bent as you see. Got my knees bent with standing so long . . .' The report concluded 'that a large mass of deformity had been produced at Bradford by the factory system'. Richard Oastler, whose statue,

Oastler statue

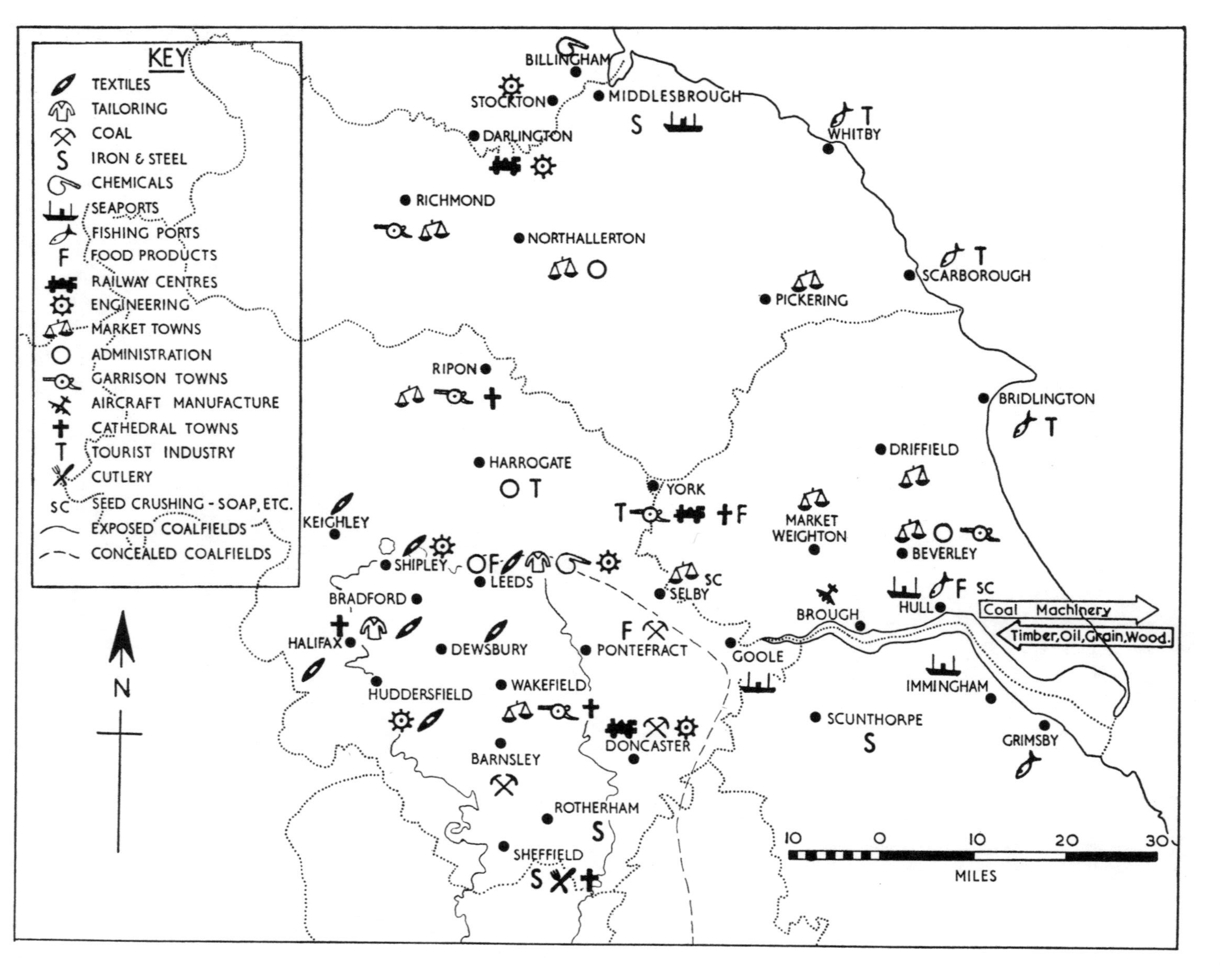

Map 12. Yorkshire Industry *c.* 1950.

surrounded by those of the children for whom he fought, stands near the centre of Bradford, was one of the reformers who attacked the employers of child labour. In 1830 he wrote to the *Leeds Mercury* the first of his letters on 'Slavery in Yorkshire', in which he described the children who hastened 'half-dressed, but not half-fed, to the Worsted Mills'.

'Short Time Committees' were set up in Yorkshire to mobilise public opinion against the factory conditions. The committees soon began to agitate against the Poor Law Amendment Act of 1834, under which the system of outdoor relief administered by the Parish Vestry was gradually replaced by the Workhouse, administered by Commissioners. Richard Oastler, along with the Rev. J. Stephens, the Rev. G.S. Bull and Feargus O'Connor led the protests. Strong oratory was soon matched by demonstrations to halt the meetings of local Poor Law Guardians in Bradford, Keighley, Dewsbury and Todmorden, but the New Poor Law was eventually enforced. The Board of Guardians was established in Leeds in 1844, 10 years after the Act was passed.

Many of the people who protested against the New Poor Law were weavers who continued their radicalism with the Chartist movement. The Chartists' campaign for parliamentary representation for the working class had strong roots amongst workers in Yorkshire, where the leaders supported physical force as a means of achieving their aims. Feargus O'Connor edited the Chartist newspaper *The Northern Star* in Leeds, which had a weekly circulation of 50,000 copies by 1839. One of the largest Chartist demonstrations was on Whit Monday 1839 at Peep Green, when a crowd of 200,000 people was addressed by O'Connor. Chartism collapsed after 1848 but many of its supporters led the development of the trade union and co-operative movement in Yorkshire.

Mid-Victorian prosperity, typified by the Great Exhibition of 1851 at Crystal Palace, was created in the mills and factories of the north of England and not least by the manufacturing industries of Yorkshire. One of the largest exhibition areas at Crystal Palace was the 'Sheffield Court', which included displays of Sheffield cutlery and edge tools. Yet such prosperity was mingled with hardship. In the 1860s as many as a fifth of union members in the Sheffield trades were out of work and supported by union funds. Pressure to maintain union subscriptions led to outbreaks of violence in Sheffield, but generally trade unionism was becoming more respectable as craft unions organised their own friendly society benefits and sought to improve their working conditions.

Many trade unionists began to appreciate that if they were to achieve genuine political representation for working class people it would have to be through an independent working class party. The Bradford Manningham Mills strike of 1890 and 1891, which ended in defeat when the strikers finally accepted wage reductions imposed by the management, led many unionists to turn from the Liberal Party which they had come to support. The Independent Labour Party emerged out of the strike and held its first meeting in Bradford in 1893, a year after the first three

Barnsley coat of arms

independent Labour M.P.s had been elected, one of whom was the seamen's leader, James Havelock Wilson, who became M.P. for Middlesbrough.

The course of the Industrial Revolution in Yorkshire ran unevenly. Old trades and customs often continued alongside new manufacturing processes. Boom towns grew rapidly but still suffered depressions of trade. However, with the growth of economic status came municipal pride. While great towns like Leeds, Hull and York had for centuries enjoyed the right to self-government, the new towns, as they burgeoned into great cities, were given councils and mayors. The Municipal Borough of Sheffield was created in 1843; that of Bradford in 1847 and Middlesbrough in 1853.

The new councils were empowered to control water supplies, police, street lighting and health. Later other responsibilities such as education were taken on. Private individuals sometimes took it upon themselves to improve the conditions of their fellow citizens. The most important example in Yorkshire was that of Sir Titus Salt, the inventor of a process for spinning and weaving alpaca. His model village, built next to his mills at Saltaire in Shipley in the 1850s, provided decent houses and open spaces for his workers. Others, like John Wilhelm Rowntree in York, took an interest in Adult Education, building on the popularity of the Mechanics' Institutes, of which the first was founded in Leeds in 1824.

While the impact of the Industrial Revolution would eventually be felt in every part of the county, large tracts of land, not only in the Dales but in the Vale of York and elsewhere, did not succumb to the ravages of industrial manufacture. The combination of industry and countryside still continues.

Hand spinning wheel

34. Leeds Town Hall after being restored to its Victorian splendour in 1972. Built by Cuthbert Brodrick in 1858.

35. Toll bridge over the Ouse at Selby, dating from 1791.

36. Launch of the *Hebridean Isles* at Cochrane's shipyard in Selby by the Duchess of Kent.

37. Five-Rise Locks, Bingley. Opened in 1774, they raise the canal level by 59 feet.

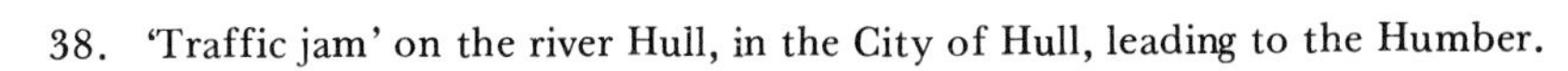

38. 'Traffic jam' on the river Hull, in the City of Hull, leading to the Humber.

39. The Bramhope railway tunnel memorial in Otley churchyard.

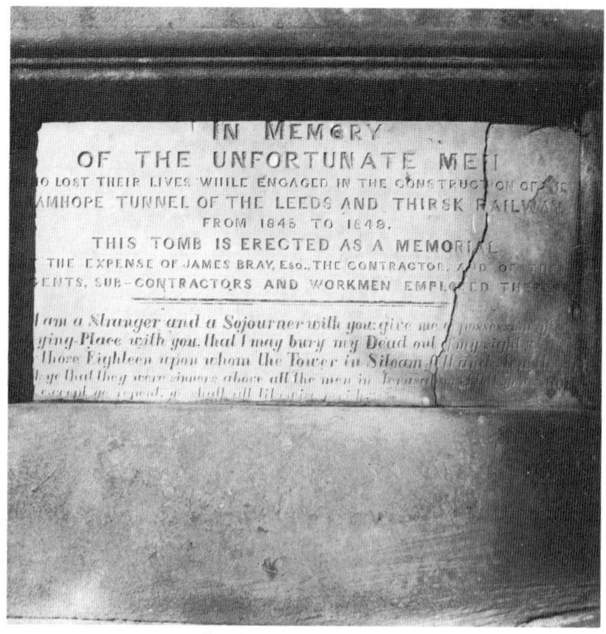

40. Memorial to the men killed while constructing the Bramhope tunnel between 1845 and 1849.

41. The Ribblehead viaduct on the Settle to Carlisle line. The line is now under threat of closure.

XV Yorkshire Transport: Roads

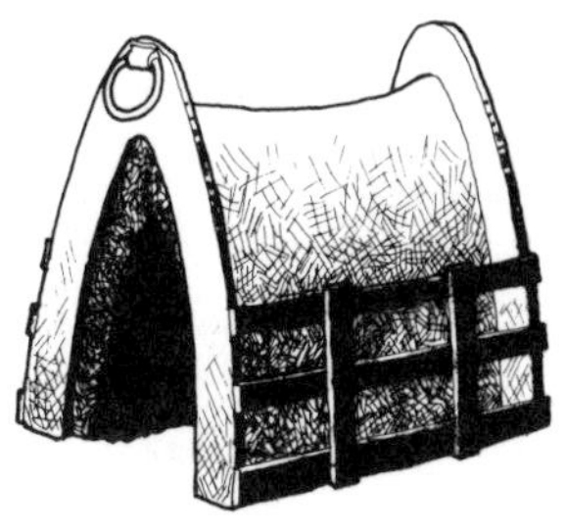

Packhorse saddle

The rapid growth of industry in Yorkshire could not have occurred unless it had been accompanied by an improvement in communications. The road system which was a legacy of the Romans was supplemented during the Middle Ages by pack-horse tracks linking the market centres; and sometimes tracks would be made to navigable stretches of rivers. The drovers' roads, used by the monks in the Middle Ages and by Scottish cattle herders in more recent times, traversed the open Pennine moorlands, away from the rising industrial centres.

When the West Riding woollen trade began to expand in the 16th century, a new network of pack-horse tracks was laid down, linking the upland areas of the Pennines with textile towns such as Halifax and Wakefield. The tracks were adequate for the transport of small quantities of cloth, but were not suitable for wheeled carts, and became increasingly inadequate when the iron industry began to develop, requiring heavier and more frequent loads of fuel and raw materials.

The great obstacle to safe wheeled transport was the condition of the roads, which were usually without any foundations or any means of drainage. Flooded roads, a particular problem in the low-lying areas of Holderness, isolated many villages in winter. People were loath to be responsible for improvements to a road passing through their village if the only beneficiaries were strangers making their way to a distant town. Long journeys were not only made hazardous by the conditions of the roads but also by the chance of being held up by highwaymen, who bore no resemblance to the fanciful portrayals to be found in books and films. One famous 17th-century highwayman was Dick Turpin, alias 'Swift Nick', who was born at Pontefract and was credited with riding from Gravesend to York in a day.

There was no incentive to keep roads in good condition until the 17th and 18th centuries, when Parliament made local turnpike trusts responsible for the construction and maintenance of specified lengths of road. The trusts were formed by groups of people who were allowed to charge travellers for using the road. The income not only paid for the cost of the road and its upkeep but enabled dividends to be paid to the shareholders. The first Yorkshire turnpike, opened in 1735, was on the Blackstone Edge road linking Halifax with Rochdale in Lancashire, though turnpikes were established on parts of the Great North road as early as 1663. The first turnpike in the East Riding linked Beverley with Woodmansey, Dunswell and Newlands, north of Hull, in 1774.

Milestone

The increase in turnpikes was related to the growth of industry, especially in the West Riding, where improved roads were essential for the transport of wool and other goods. The road from Kendal to Keighley and Halifax was improved by a turnpike trust so that larger quantities of wool could be transported more quickly from Westmorland and Craven to the clothiers at Halifax market. The road linked Skipton with Kirkby Lonsdale and joined the Halifax turnpike at Keighley, making the transport of wool more reliable and contributing to the growth of Skipton, which became the collection point for Craven wool.

Another town which grew as a result of a new turnpike was Scarborough, where spa wells had been discovered in the 1620s. The York-Scarborough turnpike was established in 1752 and from then on the town grew as a spa and a seaside resort. The same effect could be seen on Whitby, which had little connection with inland areas of Yorkshire. In 1765 the town was connected to York by turnpike, enabling it to diversify its economy, which had previously been dominated by the sea.

Although the new turnpikes brought many benefits they did not please everyone. Hull and York gained at the expense of smaller market towns like Beverley and Malton, which could not compete with the expanding trade of the larger markets. The turnpikes were avoided by many people, such as drovers who ceased to use the Great North Road because of the expense. Often the creation of a turnpike was opposed by locals who dismantled the toll gates. After an attack on the turnpike at Harewood, where 30 people were arrested, an angry crowd marched to Leeds, where they fought troops who had been called from York. Before the riot was over eight people had been killed and many others injured.

The turnpikes encouraged experiments in different methods of road making. John Metcalf, known as 'Blind Jack of Knaresborough', was one of the most famous of the early road builders. Blinded at the age of six, Metcalf nevertheless continued to lead a full and active life. In 1765 he was employed by a turnpike trust to reconstruct the Boroughbridge to Knaresborough road. He supervised every aspect of the work, including the delivery of provisions for his workers. The method usually employed by Metcalf was to put down layers of heather, sometimes known as 'ling', to provide a foundation for stone and rubble quarried from the local area. This method was used to great effect in building the road across Pule Moss for the trustees of the Wakefield to Austerlande Turnpike, which forms part of the route from Wakefield to Manchester, where the usual stone foundation would have sunk into the mire. Metcalf constructed roads in many parts of Yorkshire between 1755 and 1780 and his methods influenced the work of George Stephenson when he built the Manchester to Liverpool railway over Chat Moss.

Blind Jack of Knaresboro'

Another road builder who worked in Yorkshire was John Loudon Macadam, who first built roads for the Board of Agriculture so that the transport of food could be improved. Macadam laid a foundation of rubble on which a layer of angular blocks of stone was compressed. This method was used on the White Cross turnpike in 1820. Both Metcalf's and Macadam's methods produced a firm convex surface,

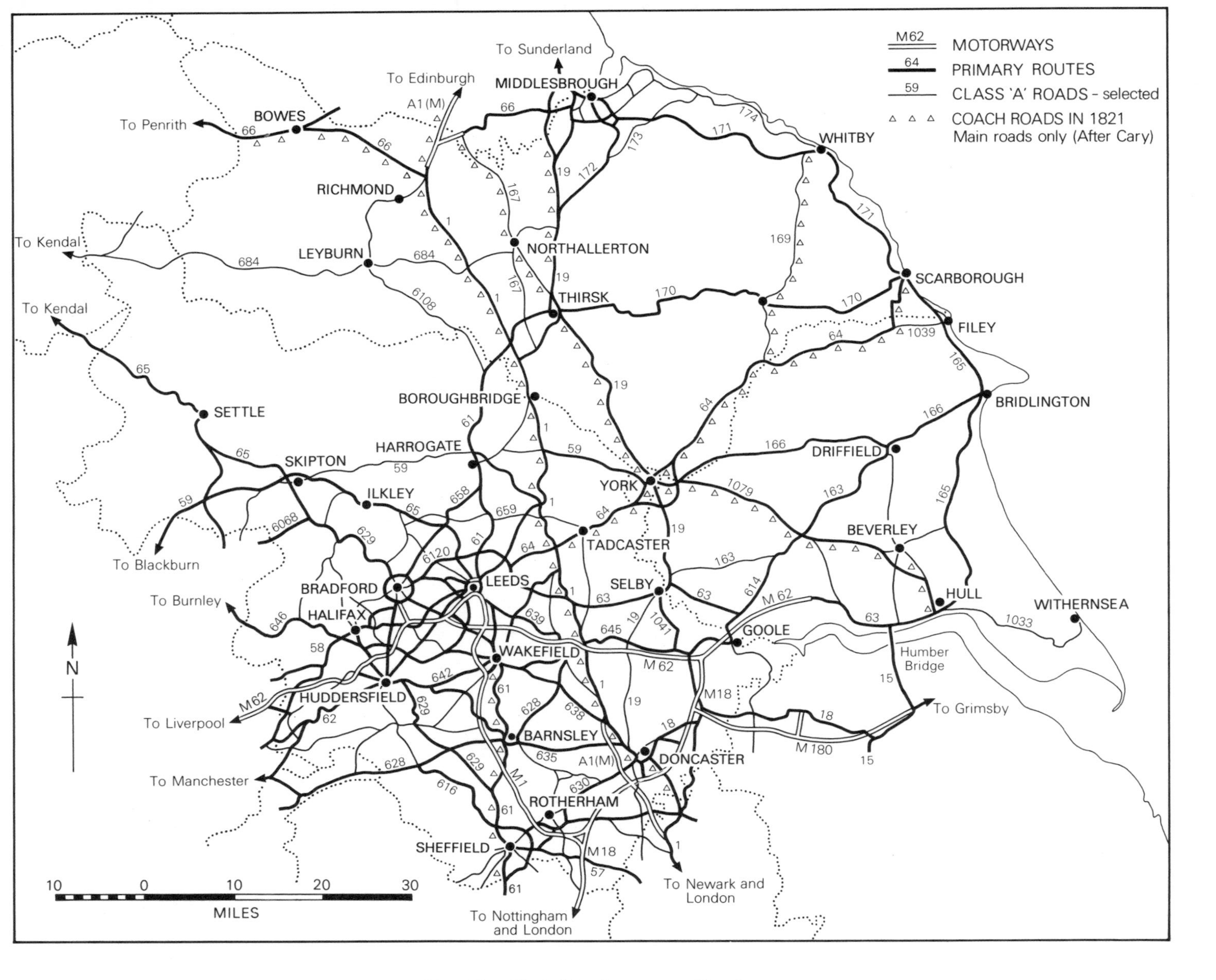

Map 13. Yorkshire Transport: Roads.

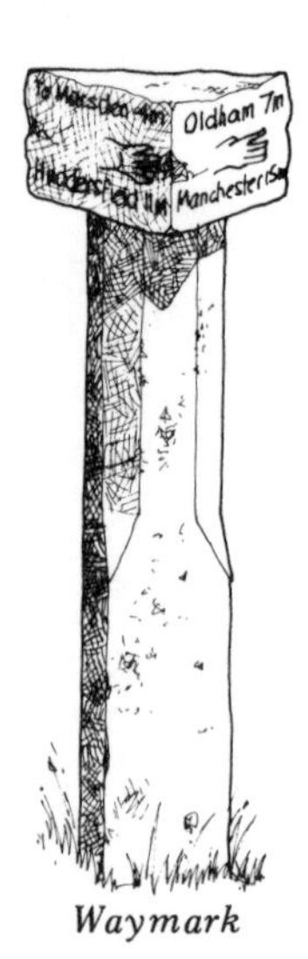

Waymark

facilitating drainage. As a result of these improvements both the volume and the speed of traffic increased, aided by the invention of the 'flying coach' with sprung suspension. The fastest of these were mail coaches which could travel at an average speed of eight m.p.h. A journey from York to Leeds took three hours compared with eight hours before road improvement. At the beginning of the 18th century travellers from Leeds to London would be on the road for a hazardous four days, riding by horseback to Wakefield, where they would board a coach travelling down the Great North Road. By 1785 this journey had been reduced to 26 hours – the time it took for the first Royal Mail coach to reach the *Bull and Mouth* in London from the *Old King's Arms* in Leeds.

The heyday of the coaching trade was the 1830s, but within 10 years it was ruined by competition from the railways. The opening of the York to Scarborough railway in 1846 and the building of a line to Pickering to link with the railway to Whitby destroyed the turnpikes which had first realised the trading and tourist potential of seaside towns. The York-Scarborough Turnpike trustees ceased collecting tolls in 1865 and the toll bars were dismantled. While some turnpike trustees were astute enough to hold shares in competing railway schemes, others attempted to protect their turnpikes by combining with others in a union of trusts which levied a common toll. However such efforts could only delay the abolition of turnpikes, at which point local parishes once again took responsibility for their upkeep. In 1888 the parishes handed over maintenance of 'main' roads to the newly formed county councils.

The next major development of roads in Yorkshire occurred after the Second World War. In 1946 proposals were put forward for a 'comprehensive reconstruction of the principal national routes' which included a motorway crossing the Pennines from south Lancashire to Hull and the conversion of parts of the Great North Road into motorways, with by-passes taking the road away from town centres. When the roads were finally built, in the 1960s and 1970s, they significantly altered the landscape in many parts of Yorkshire. The M1 motorway was extended northwards to Leeds and when the M62 motorway was opened it followed the original trans-Pennine route, making it the country's highest motorway, opening up glorious views of the Pennines to millions of travellers. One of Britain's first urban motorways was the Leeds Inner City Ring Road, which illustrates how a city landscape can be radically altered through road development. However, there is an increasing awareness of the effects of road building on the environment. The Secretary of State for the Environment summed up the change in attitudes and policy when, in 1975, he overruled the report of a public enquiry which had recommended acceptance of a proposal by the City of York for an inner ring road running close to the City's Roman Wall. However the architecture of modern road construction, particularly in the case of bridges, can sometimes be pleasing to the eye. The Humber Bridge, with the world's longest bridge span of 4,626 ft., is a spectacular example of modern road engineering.

Jowett Jupiter car

XVI Yorkshire Transport: Navigations and Canals

Although improvements to Yorkshire's road network enabled traffic to travel faster with heavier loads, the transport of materials was still severely restricted. The growth of industry in Yorkshire necessitated the transportation of large amounts of raw materials and manufactured goods which led to the improvement and extension of the navigable stretches of rivers and also the development of a canal system.

Yorkshire is well endowed with a great river system, including the Aire, Calder, Don, Hebble, Ouse and Wharfe, which drains into the Humber. These rivers had provided a means of transport since the earliest settlements and often determined the location and development of towns and cities. The rivers were very important in medieval Yorkshire and were used, for example, for the transport of stone for York Minster and for many of the great monasteries located near the banks of rivers. The River Ouse was used to import materials for local industries – alum, madder and woad for the production of cloth; iron and lead for smelting – and produce for domestic consumption, including grain, spices, wine and salted fish, and also coal for fires.

Most of the river improvements occurred in the 18th century when good transport became a major factor in the industrial development of the West Riding, and by the end of the century most of the river traffic had shifted to the south and west of Yorkshire at the expense of rivers further north. Under an Act of 1699 the proprietors of the Aire and Calder Navigation were empowered to improve the Aire as far as Leeds and the Calder to Wakefield, connecting both towns with Hull via the Ouse and Humber. The River Derwent was made navigable under an Act of 1702, which allowed shipments of corn to reach Hull from Malton. In 1726 an Act permitting improvements to the River Don enabled the Sheffield cutlers to import high grade Swedish iron ore.

River navigation could not solve all the transport problems of industrial Yorkshire, and so artificial waterways – canals – were cut into the landscape. The canals were the largest engineering constructions ever seen in Yorkshire and required materials and labour on an unprecedented scale. Three canals, the Leeds-Liverpool, the Rochdale and the Huddersfield Narrow Canal, cross the Pennines into Lancashire. The most impressive of these is the Leeds-Liverpool canal, which took 46 years to complete from the time work started in 1770. The line of the canal, over 108 miles long, was laid out along the Aire Valley by James Brindley, one of the greatest of the canal builders, who also designed the flights of locks which raised or lowered the canal boats on to different levels. One of these flights, the Bingley Five Rise lock, alters the height of the water by 59 ft. 2 ins. and is the most impressive in Britain. The canal crosses the Pennines through the 1,640-yard Foulridge tunnel at Colne (the 5,456-yard Standedge tunnel, carrying the Huddersfield Canal through to Lancashire is the longest in Yorkshire) and the water level of the whole system is maintained by supplies from seven specially-built reservoirs, holding a total of 1,200 million gallons. The canal was linked to Bradford by the Bradford Canal which, although only measuring three miles, made an enormous difference to the development of Bradford as the centre of the worsted textile industry. The Leeds-Liverpool canal joined the Aire and Calder Navigation at Leeds, enabling traffic to continue through to the East Coast via the Ouse and the Humber. The lower Aire, however, could not deal with the increasing volume of trade and so a canal linking Knottingley with Goole was opened in 1826. This canal greatly improved the means of exporting coal from the rich south Yorkshire coal seams and led to the rapid expansion of the Yorkshire coal industry. Goole had previously been a small hamlet at the lower end of the Ouse, close to the Humber; it now became the focal point of most of the Yorkshire navigation and canal system, achieving the status of a foreign trade port in 1828.

The River Don Navigation – named the Dutch River after the Dutchman Cornelius Vermuyden who drained and reclaimed tracts of land in the area in the 1620s – also flows into the River Ouse at Goole, providing a link between Sheffield, Doncaster and the Humber. The River Derwent, flowing through Malton and reaching the Ouse between Selby and Goole, was made navigable as early as 1720 and enabled the export of corn from the East Riding, with lime and coal being taken upstream. Most goods were transported by the Yorkshire Keel – a small sailing barge which could be seen on the River Ouse until the Second World War. The Market Weighton canal and the Driffield Navigation were also built in the East Riding, but these, like many other stretches of inland waterways in Yorkshire, are no longer used by goods traffic.

The great age of canal building – the period of 'canal mania' – was between 1750 and 1830, when most of the Yorkshire canals were completed. The workmen engaged on the construction of the canals were known as 'navvies' because they built 'navigations', and were often engaged in dangerous work. The report of 'a stranger called Thomas Jones supposed from Shropshire, having been unfortunately killed in the works near Gannow by a fall', which was made to the Leeds and Liverpool Canal Company in 1800, was an indication of the risks the men often had to take. Many of the navvies came from Ireland and

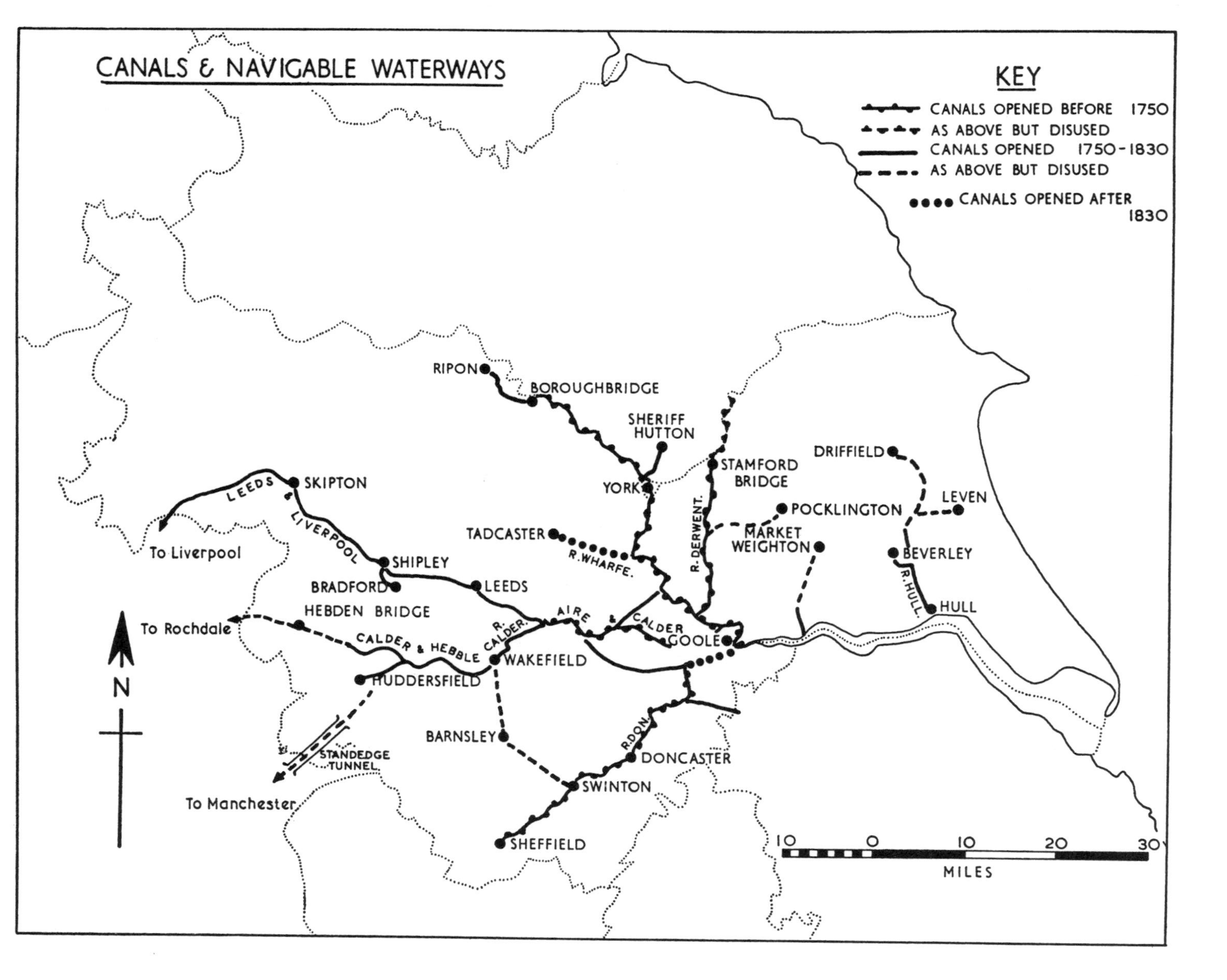

Map 14. Yorkshire Transport: Canals and Navigations.

Scotland seeking jobs and lived a nomadic life travelling from one construction site to the next, often living in primitive conditions.

The canals provided employment for people who lived as well as worked on the canal barges. Life on the canal was not easy; men often had to tow the barges themselves if there was no suitable tow-path to allow horses to do the work. The tow-path did not continue through tunnels, so men called 'leggers' had to lay on a plank extending from the side of the barge to the tunnel wall. In this position the legger would 'walk' along the side or roof of the canal, to propel the barge.

The canals were especially suitable for the bulk transport of raw materials, since a barge drawn by a horse could carry 30 tons compared with two hundredweight by a pack horse or half a ton by waggon. Cheaper and more regular food supplies were made available to the rapidly expanding urban populations of the West Riding, while lime and building stone, in great demand for the building of mills and houses, could be transported from quarries further afield. The Leeds-Liverpool canal became the arterial route for the movement of textiles in and out of the West Riding. Imported raw wool destined for Bradford was loaded onto barges at Liverpool, whence consignments of finished woollen cloth were shipped abroad. In 1834 the Yorkshire section of the canal carried over 100,000 tons of coal, compared with 17,500 tons in 1784. The first barge to arrive in Skipton on the opening of the Bingley-Skipton section of the canal in 1773 carried coal which was sold at half its normal price.

The development of the railway system was to bring an end to most of the commercial traffic on Yorkshire canals. While barges could carry more weight than packhorses, they could not compete with the loads and speed of the train. The Leeds-Liverpool Canal Company tried to restrict the effects of competition by giving railway companies the right to collect certain canal dues in return for a fixed income. However such measures could only delay the end of the canal age. By the 1840s all three trans-Pennine canals were suffering from railway competition. The canal traffic to Selby and Goole was affected by the building of the Leeds-Selby railway line which connected with a fast river steam packet service to Hull. The line opened in 1834 forcing the Aire and Calder Navigation to reduce canal tolls by an average of 40 per cent.

The canals in Yorkshire continued to decline, though it was not until after the First World War that the full impact of the railways and, later, motorised road transport, began to be felt. The Bradford Canal was still handling over 100,000 tons of freight a year in the 1900s, but this had fallen to only 28,000 tons by 1920, and two years later it was closed and later filled in. However, many of the canals in Yorkshire still continue to be used, though most of the traffic, such as that on the Leeds-Liverpool Canal, consists of leisure craft. It could be argued that the great age of canal building has left us with the only transport system that actually enhances our appreciation of the landscape; certainly the great canals that can still be seen in Yorkshire are appreciated by Yorkshire people and visitors alike.

42. Andrew Marvell (1621-78), poet, satirist and pamphleteer, who became M.P. for Hull and foreign language secretary to Oliver Cromwell.

43. William Wilberforce (1759-1833) was educated at Hull Grammar School, became Tory M.P. for Hull in 1780 and M.P. for Yorkshire in 1784. He led the anti-slavery campaign and learned of the second reading of a bill to abolish slavery shortly before he died.

44. Sir Titus Salt (1803-76), Mayor of Bradford, founder of Saltaire industrial village, and pioneer textile manufacturer.

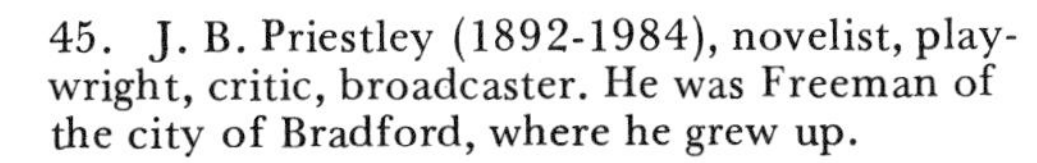

45. J. B. Priestley (1892-1984), novelist, playwright, critic, broadcaster. He was Freeman of the city of Bradford, where he grew up.

46. Boulder Clough chapel, Sowerby, 1898.

47. The Methodist chapel at Heptonstall, reputed to be the oldest in the world still in regular use. John Wesley preached there.

48. Heathcote, Ilkley, designed by Sir Edwin Lutyens, 1906.

49. The Alhambra Theatre, Bradford, opened in 1914 and restored in 1986.

50. Victorian Leeds: Thornton's shopping arcade, Briggate, 1878.

51. Sculptor Henry Moore talking to children in his home town of Castleford, where he positioned his sculpture outside the Civic Centre.

52. Fairburn Inngs Nature Reserve, near Castleford, West Yorkshire, created on land affected by mining subsidence.

XVII Yorkshire Transport: Railways

Blenkinsop's engine

Although railways began to supersede the canal transport system in the 1840s, a rail network had in fact begun to emerge much earlier. The first 'railway' in Yorkshire was built by Charles Brandling, a Leeds colliery owner, who secured an Act of Parliament in 1758 to construct a waggonway on an incline connecting his colliery in Middleton to Old Staithes on the River Aire, via Hunslet Moor. The waggons were originally hauled up the incline by horses, which were later replaced by a fixed steam engine, until John Blenkinsop, an employee of Brandling's, experimented with a steam engine design by Richard Trevithick. The engine used a rack and pinion method to haul the coal waggons and began regular service in 1812 with two steam engines, the *Salamanca* and the *Prince Regent*, hauling 38 fully laden waggons at a speed of three m.p.h.

Brandling's railway aroused great interest and was visited by George Stephenson, who was later to build the world's first passenger railway, and by the Grand Duke Nicholas of Russia. The economic value of the railway was quickly realised and Brandling was able to secure control of the coal supplies to Leeds. One of the drawbacks was that a great deal of iron – 30 lb. for every yard – was used to construct the rack and pinion rail, resulting in a cost per mile almost as great as the total cost of a steam engine (the *Prince Regent*, built at Hunslet, cost £380). Other coal owners in Yorkshire began to follow Brandling's lead and many waggonways were constructed, sometimes on inclined wooden tracks. In Bradford, for example, several waggonways carrying waggons hauled by horse and pulley were constructed in the 1780s, connecting coal pits and iron works with the Bradford Canal.

A viable public railway system did not exist until 1825, when George Stephenson built a railway running from Stockton to Darlington. An extension of this railway was opened to Middlesbrough in 1830 making it the first public steam-worked railway in Yorkshire.

We have already noted how, by the 1830s, the industrial expansion of the West Riding was being held back by increasingly inadequate transport facilities. The building of the Knottingley-Goole canal had eased some of the problems but at the same time had damaged the trading status of Selby. A railway from Leeds to Selby had been advocated as early as 1802 and the first detailed plan for the line was put forward in 1821; this plan was shelved, mainly because no-one could resolve the question of what sort of locomotive power should be employed. The plan was resurrected in 1829, by which time the steam engine was being successfully used on a number of lines. Even so the promoters of the line considered using horses to pull the railway waggons, before choosing steam engines. The Pickering-Whitby line, opened in 1836, continued to use horses as a means of locomotion until 1847. When the Leeds-Selby line opened in 1834 it was the first public railway to operate wholly within Yorkshire. The building of the railway and its operation highlighted the competition taking place between canals and railways, although the relationship between the different forms of transport was at first ambiguous; the Leeds-Selby line, while competing with the Knottingley-Goole canal, nevertheless only existed because of its dependence on the river trade from the Ouse and down the Humber to Hull. The railways, carrying thousands of passengers each week by the 1840s, also competed with the turnpike, though stage coach operators benefited by transporting passengers to and from the railway stations. Passengers on the Leeds-Selby line were the first in the world to travel by steam locomotive through a tunnel – the 637 m.-long (700 yds.) Richmond Hill tunnel at Marsh Lane. By 1840 the line had been extended to Hull, thus eliminating the need for connecting river transport.

People quickly began to realise the importance of railways; not only were they a better form of transport – heavier loads could be carried faster at cheaper rates than by road or canal and the public could travel in greater comfort – they also opened up new markets for goods and created a great demand for iron and steel and other products in their construction. They also required a great deal of labour, both in the building and maintenance of the railway system and in other industries which benefited from improved transport. By the 1840s finance for new railway lines was easier to find, and thousands of small investors were placing their money with schemes which had little hope of making money. The greatest rush to build, between 1845 and 1847, was known as 'railway mania'. In 1847, 76 Bills were presented to Parliament for schemes affecting Yorkshire and by 1860 most of the modern railway network in the county had been completed. By the end of the 1840s both York and Leeds were connected to most major towns and cities in the country. Bradford, by means of two rail links to Leeds, was also connected to the network.

Leeds Northern Railway Co. badge

The railway competition was so fierce that some towns in Yorkshire were served by several lines. Leeds had three stations, Sheffield and Bradford had two each and even Pontefract had three to itself. The largest scheme to be proposed was the Great Northern Railway running from London to Doncaster which aroused intense opposition from George Hudson, the 'Railway King', who rose to fame when he tried to establish York as a major railway centre. Hudson, who already had an East Coast route which would be affected by the Great Northern, strongly objected

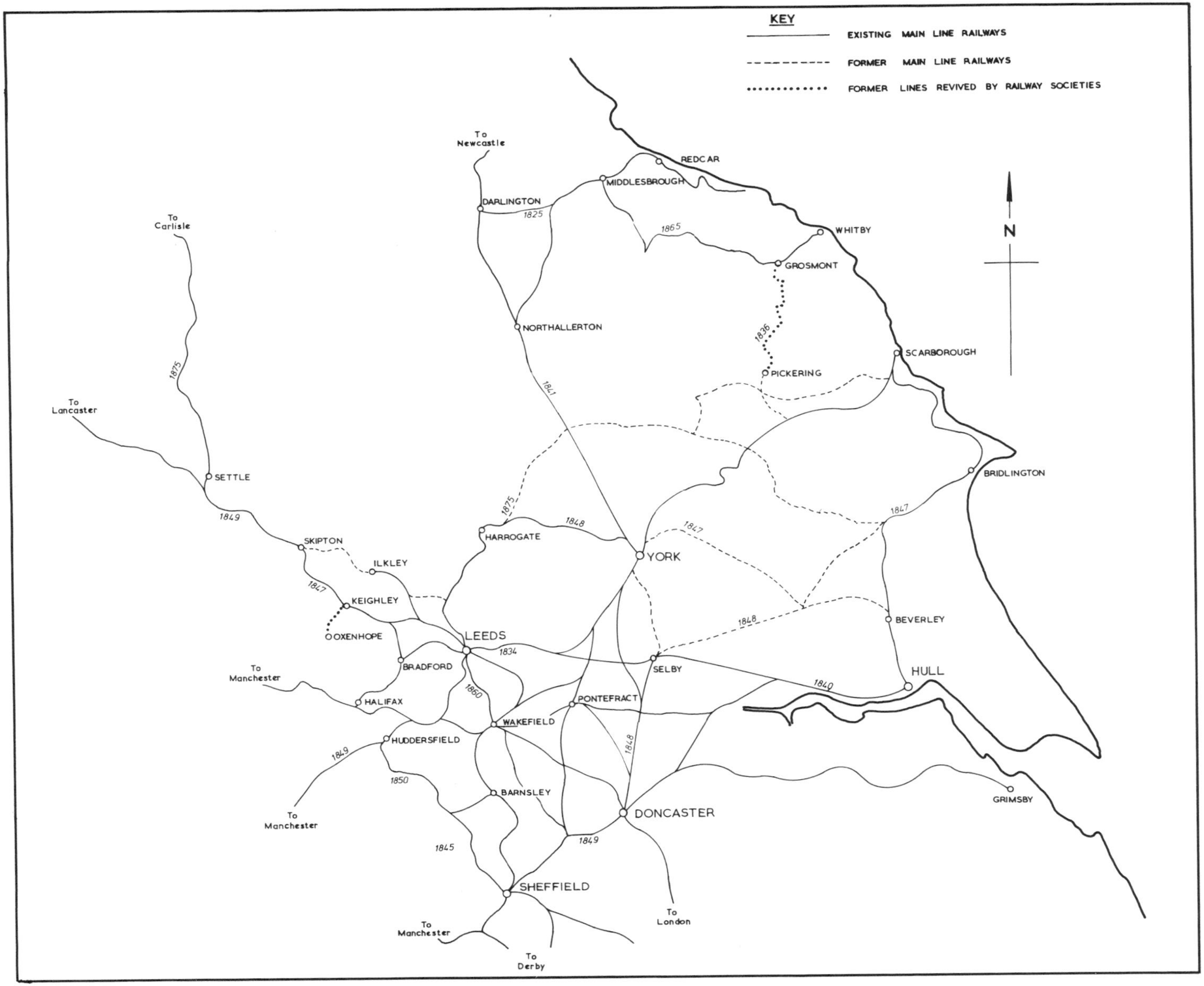

Map 15. Yorkshire Transport: Railways.

'Contractors' hotel'

but to no avail. The Great Northern then had to contend with the four major companies in the West Riding – the London & North Western, the Lancashire & Yorkshire, the Midland, and the Manchester, Sheffield & Lincolnshire Railway – which combined to try to force it out of business. This attempt also failed and the Great Northern became one of the foremost railway companies in the country.

George Hudson confused his private business interests with his public office (he was three times Lord Mayor of York) and went to extraordinary lengths to outwit competitors. He paid £470,000 to the 6th Duke of Devonshire for his 12,000-acre Londesborough estate in the East Riding to prevent all other railway companies from building lines to Hull, before selling part of it back to his own company so that he could build his own line. When he took charge of the North Midland Railway objections were raised that he cut wages and salaries; he responded by sacking the protestors without notice on Christmas Eve. Such tactics did not endear him to the public, but as long as his companies paid good dividends few would complain. When railway profits began to fall, Hudson's methods were more carefully scrutinised and his corrupt practices were exposed. The lasting benefit of George Hudson's work was the amalgamation of many small lines into larger companies, culminating in the formation of the North Eastern Railway in 1854.

By the end of 'railway mania' Yorkshire had a comprehensive railway system, but it was established as much by the principles of greed and avarice as by the need to provide a rational system of transport and communication. The services offered by the railway companies gradually improved; open third-class carriages were no longer to be seen; upholstered seats and improved suspension and brakes became quite common. More lines were built in Yorkshire in the 1860s and 1870s extending into more rural areas. When the line along Wharfedale was opened in 1865 the villages and towns along its route began to expand, especially Ilkley, where many Bradford businessmen began to build their homes. In 1866 the Midland company applied for permission to build a line from Settle to Carlisle via Ribblesdale and the Eden valley. When the line was opened in 1875 it had cost a total of £3,500,000 and involved great feats of engineering, including a one-and-a-half mile tunnel cutting 500 ft. under Blea Moor and also the Ribblehead viaduct. It is perhaps the most interesting and certainly the highest main-line in England, rising to 1,169 ft. at the Aisgill summit. The Hull and Barnsley Railway, opened in 1885, linked the south Yorkshire coalfields with Alexandra Docks in Hull, and also provided improved passenger access for villages in the Yorkshire Wolds and Howdenshire. The Hull and Barnsley Company was amalgamated with the North Eastern in 1922 and the line was closed in stages between 1959 and 1964. A small section of the high level line through Hull remains open to convey Hull City Football Club supporters from the city centre to their team's home ground at Boothferry Park.

Bog cart

The building of the railways attracted thousands of navvies to Yorkshire, many of whom came from Ireland. When the Settle to Carlisle line was built the men were housed in shanty towns named after far away places – Sebastopol, Jericho, Salt Lake City etc. – which sprang up along the route. The navvies left when the building work was complete, leaving behind the farming communities which must have experienced quite a shock on their arrival.

The subsequent history of Yorkshire's railways is one of amalgamation, consolidation and, finally, contraction. The North-Eastern Railway Company had absorbed over 50 smaller companies by 1914. A Railways Act of 1921 divided the companies into four groups, the Great Western, the Southern, the London & North-Eastern, and the London, Midland & Scottish, the latter two operating most of the lines in Yorkshire. A Railway Rates Tribunal fixed charges based on earnings in 1913, although none of the companies achieved their pre-war levels of income.

The First World War was in fact a watershed for the railways. Motorised road transport enabled motor-buses and private cars to compete with short-distance rail passenger traffic, while road hauliers, able to deliver goods straight to the door, began to take business away from railway goods traffic. By the mid-1930s road transport had taken half the traffic away from the railways and the total workforce had fallen by 18 per cent. The railways were nationalised after the Second World War and in 1963 the Beeching report recommended a major reorganisation of the network involving the closure of thousands of miles of track. Many of the rural lines in Yorkshire were closed and the emphasis was placed on rapid urban and inter-city services.

The railway network in Yorkshire is now much reduced from the vast array of tracks laid down in the 19th century. Diesel Multiple Units are a common sight on most lines in the region and inter-city services link the major towns and cities with the rest of the country. The travel time from Leeds to London has been reduced to 2 hours 9 minutes. Some steam trains, however, still run, carrying rail enthusiasts on special excursions, such as those from Leeds and York to Scarborough. The importance of York as a railway centre is remembered in the Railway Museum which attracts thousands of visitors each year. In the summer months special Dalesrail excursions are organised from Leeds and Bradford along the Settle-Carlisle line and tourists and hikers fill the trains each weekend. Some of the disused lines have been taken over by preservation groups which run them as tourist attractions. The Worth Valley railway, running from Haworth to Keighley, is sometimes used by film companies because of its scenic qualities, and steam trains are run on the line across the North York Moors between Pickering and Grosmont.

Hercules *engine*

XVIII Yorkshire after the Industrial Revolution

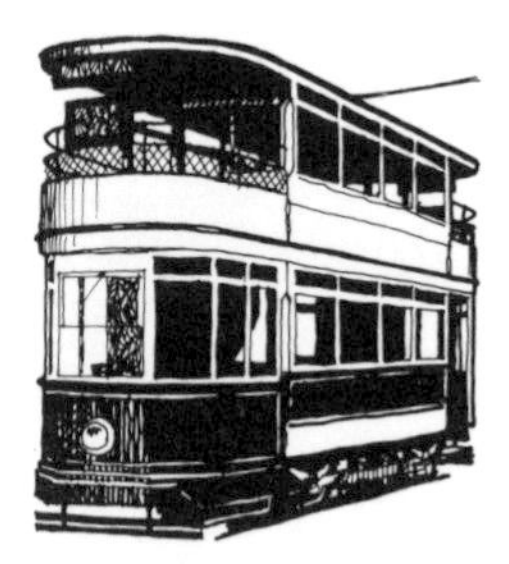

Bradford's last tram

The industries which formed the base of the Industrial Revolution in Yorkshire – textiles, coal, iron and steel etc, – continued to develop throughout the 19th century, although it was increasingly apparent that the rapid early rates of growth could not be sustained. In the case of the West Riding woollen industry the most affluent period was between 1860 and 1874. In the last quarter of the century the industry suffered a decline because of foreign competition, particularly from France, poor textile design and difficulties in the supply of wool. The introduction of protective tariffs, mainly by France and America, also severely affected the trade. In Leeds the staple trades of cloth and flax were suffering as early as 1850.

In spite of periodic trade depressions, however, changes in the manufacturing base made Yorkshire a region of high economic growth until the outbreak of the First World War. While the old industries were experiencing problems, other industries were expanding. In Leeds the engineering, chemical and leather industries all employed more people, and the relatively new industries of footwear and printing ensured the continued growth of the local economy, which by the First World War had become much more diverse.

Economic prosperity did not necessarily mean that conditions of work or social life in Yorkshire were always improving. In the second half of the 19th century many trade unions joined local trades councils in order to protect workers in local disputes and also to campaign against government legislation which affected the rights of workers. By the late 1880s a more militant form of trade unionism was beginning to emerge, based mainly on the craft unions. The textile unions, for example, were strengthened as a result of the Manningham Mills strike (Chapter XIV); earlier, in 1881, two miners' unions had joined together to form the Yorkshire Miners Association, which was to be instrumental in the formation of the Miners Federation of Great Britain. One of the most bitter industrial disputes of the 1890s involved the Yorkshire miners. In 1893 Yorkshire coal owners tried to impose substantial wage reductions; when these were rejected, the miners were locked out, resulting in hardship and poverty amongst the families of the 50,000 miners. Blackleg miners, who added to the sense of grievance, were attacked and coal mine property was burned down. The most serious incident was at Featherstone on 7 September 1893, when the army fired shots into a crowd of rioters who were throwing stones and attacking the colliery (owned by Lord Masham). Two miners were killed and several injured in what became known as the 'Featherstone Massacres'.

While wages were rising nationally before the war, coal miners actually suffered pay cuts, resulting in a national coal strike in 1911 which involved most of the Yorkshire pits. In 1914 a strike by Rotherham coal miners led to a five-week stoppage throughout the Yorkshire coalfield.

Social conditions in Yorkshire were still giving cause for concern. One of the most comprehensive social surveys undertaken before the First World War was that carried out by B. Seebohm Rowntree in York in 1901. Published under the title *Poverty: a Study of Town Life*, it identified 28 per cent of the population of York who lived below acceptable nutritional standards; 40 per cent of the city's schoolchildren were below this level. York was not a particularly poverty-stricken city and conditions in other towns and cities were often worse. Housing was often very poor and in the West Riding the usual living accommodation was the back-to-back house. More than a quarter of the houses were without drainage of any sort and were still being built in a similar fashion in the 1900s.

The First World War was a watershed in the industrial life of the county. Many Yorkshire workers lost their lives in the war. Leeds lost over 9,500 young men; Huddersfield almost 500, and 2,000 Bradfordians were killed on the Somme. Some east coast towns experienced enemy action – Whitby and Scarborough were bombarded by German warships.The port of Goole was badly affected when most of the port's fleet of ships was taken over by the government. The woollen industry and agriculture came under central government control, though the demands made by the war led to increased production in both industries. There was an economic boom immediately after the war which could only but disguise the way the structure and control of industry, in Yorkshire as elsewhere, had fundamentally altered.

The inter-war years in Yorkshire were marked by industrial unrest and trade depressions, but there was also a brighter picture of developments in new technology and the growth of new industries. The first signs of a slump were apparent in the early 1920s, when the major Yorkshire industries experienced stagnation and increased unemployment. The industrial disputes of the 1920s culminated in the General Strike of 1926, which did not affect Yorkshire a great deal, though there were 7,000 workers, mostly railwaymen, on strike in Leeds.

The contrasts of life in the 1930s have been amply illuminated by Bradford-born J. B. Priestley, who in his *English Journey* (published in 1934) described how members of his old battalion would not attend a re-union dinner in Bradford because they were so poor they did not have much more than rags to dress in. However it was not all depression. Bradford was still bustling with life and the woollen industry was beginning to recover, though Priestley thought it was 'now a different wool trade, with none of that easy gambling and general acceptance of good times and bad times. They snatch at every crumb of business'.

There was an increase in employment in the commercial and service sectors of the economy. Five government departments were set up in Leeds in the 1930s, helping to establish the city as an administrative centre for the county. The expansion of white-collar jobs, in which 22.7 per cent of the working population of Leeds was employed in 1931, was at the expense of jobs in manufacturing. The inter-war years saw the movement of industries and people away from Yorkshire, mainly southwards, with almost 100,000 leaving the East and West Ridings between 1921 and 1939. This process continued after the Second World War, though new jobs were also being created. In 1951, 55.4 per cent of the Leeds workforce was employed in manufacturing; by 1973 this had declined to 34.6 per cent, with a total of 37,000 manufacturing jobs lost. However almost the same number of jobs had been created in the city's service industries – banking, hotels, pubs, shops etc. – and Leeds City Council employed 34,000 people in 1975 compared with 19,000 in 1946.

The traditional economic base of Yorkshire continued to crumble after the Second World War. In the woollen textile areas 48,000 jobs were lost between 1953 and 1965. Foreign competition, for example the import of tufted carpets from America, has resulted in widespread closures. Crossley's mills in Halifax – known as 'the largest carpet factory in the world' – which employed 5,000 people in 1870, closed down as a carpet textile factory. The vast array of mills has now been converted into individual units for hundreds of small firms, many utilising modern computer technology. Many of the huge clothing factories in Leeds are now derelict (the Burton factory in Leeds employed 10,000 people in the 1930s).

A similar fate has fallen upon the coal mining industry in Yorkshire, which has suffered because of falling demand, mechanisation and the closure of 'uneconomic' pits. In the Barnsley area a multi-pit complex is replacing the old network of collieries. Automated coal preparation plants at Woolley, Grimethorpe and South Kirkby will group together a total of 16 pits. Although output will increase by 21 per cent it is expected that employment will fall by a similar amount. A vast new coalfield has been opened at Selby which will employ 3,500 people by 1988, when it is expected that 12.5 million tonnes of coal will be extracted each year, with annual profits of £170 million. The threat of contraction and redundancies in the mining industry resulted in a national miners' strike in 1984, which started in Yorkshire and lasted a full year. The miners lost their campaign to save many pits from closure and the workforce has rapidly declined.

Other industries have also suffered from a slump in trade or, like the fishing industry, have collapsed completely. In Hull, the Fishing Vessel Owners Association, which had employed 8,600 people in 1976, went into liquidation in 1980. The reasons for the collapse were the introduction of international quotas for herring and mackerel and changes in the limit of territorial waters, enabling other countries to compete in traditional British fishing grounds.

Pre-war Hull steam trawler

Yorkshire has suffered increasing economic difficulties in recent years. Unemployment is now a major problem. Between 1979 and 1981 unemployment rose by 70 per cent in the Yorkshire and Humberside region. The situation is particularly acute for young people, with 30 per cent of 16-19 year olds unemployed in Bradford, Halifax and Leeds in 1983. Some help has come to the region in the form of E.E.C. and government grants and the granting of different sorts of special area status. Science Parks have been established in various cities, linking universities with industry in the development of computer technology. Tourism is now a growth industry in the county and many of the towns and cities which experienced rapid development in the Industrial Revolution are attracting visitors. The preservation of Yorkshire's industrial past is now creating jobs in a thriving tourist industry – which would have astonished the people whose achievements in the 19th century made Yorkshire a great industrial county.

Yorkshire's last trolley-bus

XIX Leisure and Culture in Yorkshire

The cultural life of Yorkshire is very diverse and can mean different things to many people. It is possible, however, to locate general areas of cultural activity and patterns of cultural development which have determined our views of Yorkshire life. The county's pre-industrial culture, for example, was mainly rural and was broadly determined by the seasons of the year, religious festivals and the presence of a variety of animals and wildlife.

Deer hunting had been a popular sport in many areas of the Yorkshire Dales from the 12th century until large tracts of woodland were cut down for lead smelting in the 18th century, thus removing the natural habitat of the deer. Bull baiting prevailed until the 1820s, and Beverley was one of the popular centres in the 18th century, where the custom was for every newly-elected Mayor to present a bull to the town. An iron bull ring was permanently fixed to the ground at Harewood and at Skipton the local constable used to purchase the bull rope and charge it to his account. Cock fighting and stoning was another popular pastime and lasted much longer. At York the apprentices would gather to throw stones at cocks on Shrove Tuesday in the yard of the Minster. The Primitive Methodists intervened at Filey, which they described as '. . . a place noted for vice and wickedness of almost every description. Drunkenness, swearing, Sabbath-breaking, cock-fighting, card playing and dancing, have been the favourite diversions of this place for many years'.

Popular cultural activities often centred round Holy days or important dates in the agricultural year. The rural labourer knew little of regular holidays and there was still work of one sort or another to do on Christmas Day and Good Friday. There was, however, the annual feast or fair. In Darrington an annual parish feast was held when 'everybody, young and old, made merry . . . During the feast everybody kept open house; friends and relations who had left the village came back to it, sometimes from far distances, and there was a great re-union of families'. Many of the fairs, such as the Martinmas hiring fairs in the East Riding, were the continuation of old traditions which lasted until the end of the 19th century. Plough Monday was traditionally the day when work on the land resumed after Christmas and was often taken as a holiday by farm labourers, with mummers and dancing as part of the festivities. Easter week was generally a time for sport. At Richmond football

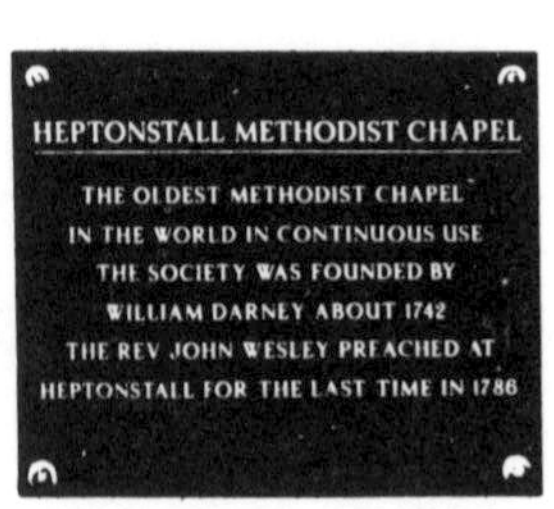

Plaque from Heptonstall Methodist chapel

and cricket were played, while in Halifax in 1681 the local preacher complained that on Easter Sunday 'as my hearers went from us through Halifax there were hundreds of people at Clark brig, in the church yard, on the green and all along the town of young people and others playing at Stool-ball [an early form of cricket] and other recreations, without any controll'.

Before the Reformation, however, the attitude of the Church had been different. For example, the development of religious drama in medieval England was an important stage in the formation of a pre-industrial culture. In York and in Wakefield, Mystery Cycles were performed by trade guilds, which were responsible for individual scenes in open-air performances of the story of man as told in the Bible. The plays were originally performed in church as part of the church litany. York was already renowned for its actors; the guilds were used to giving dramatic performances in public and touring players sometimes performed there. (As late as 1559 the President of the North, the Earl of Shrewsbury, was requested by the Earl of Leicester to allow his players to perform in Yorkshire, guaranteeing their 'honesty and good nature'.) In the mid-14th century a monk, or possibly more than one, wrote a cycle of 48 plays for various guilds which presented pageants appropriate to their craft on carts towed through the streets. The Shipwrights, for example, presented 'The Building of the Ark'; the Pinners (Nailmakers) presented Christ's Crucifixion, and the Orfevers (Goldsmiths) enacted the bearing of gifts by the three kings from the east. In Wakefield the craft guilds joined with religious guilds to perform pageants on the feast of Corpus Christi, parading through the town until all the plays were complete. The Wakefield Mystery Plays, consisting of a cycle of 32 plays, were closely connected to the York cycle until, around 1422, an unknown playwright added material which transformed the Wakefield Cycle into a brilliant piece of dramatic comedy which, with its fearsome invocations of Heaven and Hell, must have had a tremendous impact on medieval audiences. The performance of the Mystery Plays in both Wakefield and York met a communal need and became occasions of celebration and festivity.

The Reformation disrupted many of the religious as well as secular forms of celebration, and in Wakefield and in York popular forms of drama ended in the 1570s. Other factors, such as the new calendar of 1752, which did not recognise some of the old feast days, or the enclosure of common land, which affected communal patterns of work and leisure – the enclosure of common land in Pudsey ended the practice of holding a feast day on the local moor; in Hornsea local football matches ceased after enclosure in 1809 – and also the pressure to end blood sports, were each important in the evolution of Yorkshire's cultural life.

Bust of John Wesley in Heptonstall chapel

A new phase was heralded by the Industrial Revolution. In many cases traditional village life was disrupted by rapid growth into thriving industrial towns. Strangers came to live amongst the local inhabitants;

work patterns were radically altered and often mills and houses were built on open recreational spaces. Even villages which remained rural were affected by the growth of towns and cities far away, as improvements in transport and communications, and also the increasing uniformity of administrative control, broke down traditional values. The country labourer increasingly came into contact with a developing urban culture.

These developments, however, were very uneven. A correspondent to the *Morning Chronicle* in 1849 wrote of a mill owner in Saddleworth who 'told me that he had recently arranged a hunt to try the mettle of some dogs from another part of Yorkshire against the native breed. He had tried to keep the matter as quiet as he could; but it somehow leaked out, and the result was that several mills were left standing, and that more than 500 carders, slubbers, spinners and weavers formed the field. The masters, however, are often too keen sportsmen themselves to grudge their hands an occasional holiday of the sort'.

Many traditional games became formalised in new urban settings. Football and cricket, which had always been closely linked, were gradually organised into local clubs and leagues. The same ground was often used for both sports until it was realised how much damage was being caused to the surface. Sheffield Wednesday, formed in 1867, emerged from a cricket club and the Yorkshire County Cricket Club spawned Sheffield United Football club in 1889. Leeds United was founded in 1864. The Yorkshire County Cricket Club was founded in 1863 although occasional matches were played by a county team before then; in 1825 nearly 20,000 people watched an All England team defeat a Yorkshire county team by 28 runs in a match which lasted five days.

The growth of mass urban communities emphasised the need for open recreational space. When such provision was made, in the form of urban parkland, it was often by wealthy philanthropists who wished to see working people use their leisure time in certain ways and considered the park to be a means of improving social behaviour. Titus Salt, who built a model village for his mill workers at Saltaire, also provided a park nearby which opened in 1850. Organised games were allowed but anyone caught swearing, throwing stones or guilty of other 'indecorous conduct' would be excluded. The Duke of Norfolk gave a public park to the people of Sheffield in 1847. Halifax received its People's Park from Sir Frank Crossley in 1857. Some parks were provided by local corporations; Leeds purchased 63 acres of Woodhouse Moor in the 1850s for £3,000 and in 1872 bought Roundhay Park for £139,000.

Yorkshire Dales National Park symbol

The picturesque settings of Norman castles and Cistercian abbeys are part of the landscape of Yorkshire and the county's cathedrals, in particular York Minster, attract tourists in their thousands. Some great houses in the county, such as the baroque Castle Howard, built by John Vanbrugh from 1700 until his death in 1726, with a later addition by Nicholas Hawksmoor, not only attract visitors, but have also featured in films and documentaries. The architectural landscape of Yorkshire has also been shaped by the Industrial Revolution, in the form of the tough grandeur of the mills and warehouses of the West Riding. A similar legacy has been left by religious nonconformity, in the shape of vast chapels (although many are now demolished) that at one time resounded with the singing of massed choirs.

Bradford Grammar School

Most famous of the Yorkshire choirs is the Huddersfield Choral Society, founded in 1832, known particularly for its performances of Handel's *Messiah*. The choral tradition in Yorkshire developed alongside that of brass-band music and some bands, such as the Brighouse and Rastrick and the Black Dyke Mills, went on to achieve international fame. Amateur musical life was at its peak in the last 20 years of the 19th century, when in Bradford, for example, there were about fifty brass bands and choirs.

Interest in music and drama spanned both serious and popular forms and was part of a wider cultural movement fostered in part by a greater interest in self-education. Mechanics' Institutes, aimed at the education of artisans, were first established by Dr. John Birkbeck, who was born in Settle in 1776. They quickly became established in Yorkshire, most heavily concentrated in the industrial West Riding, though over 110 were established throughout the county in the 19th century. Gradually a system of higher education began to develop and the first Yorkshire universities were granted charters. The idea of a university in Leeds was originally put forward in 1826. The Yorkshire College of Science was founded there in 1874, and 10 years later a medical school was opened. A University Charter was granted in 1904. Leeds' claim to be the 'Yorkshire University' was challenged by Sheffield, where Mark Firth, a local steel master, founded a college in 1879 which was granted University status the same year as Leeds. A University College was opened in Hull in 1926 and gained its Charter in 1954. The expansion of higher education in the 1960s saw universities founded at York in 1963 and Bradford in 1964. Polytechnics were established in Huddersfield, Sheffield and Leeds and colleges now flourish throughout Yorkshire, catering for a modern multi-cultural society.

The cultural life of Yorkshire has been enriched by many people who became famous in a wider context for their contributions to the arts and sciences. The dramatist William Congreve was born at Bardsey in 1670 and Ebenezer Elliott, the 'Corn-Law Rhymer', was born at Masborough in 1781. Elliot is commemorated by a statue at Sheffield, where he died in 1841. The Bronte sisters, who were born at Thornton and later moved with their father, Patrick Bronte, to Haworth, not only wrote great literature but have also – with the more recent help of film-makers and the tourist industry – highlighted particular features of the county, such as the windswept moors of the 'Bronte Country', one of the hallmarks of our contemporary understanding of 'Yorkshire'.

Badge of Bradford University

An important contribution to 19th-century understanding of the Yorkshire countryside was made by J. M. W. Turner, considered one of the

Eight-day clock by John Bancroft of Scarborough

greatest of English painters, who made sketching tours of the county in 1816. His watercolours of Malham Cove and Gordale Scar and elsewhere evoked a public appreciation of wild romantic landscape. A rather different view of Yorkshire was painted by John Atkinson Grimshaw, who was born in Leeds in 1836. He made use of photographs to obtain the accurate detail evident in his melancholic paintings of the 19th-century industrial and commercial landscape.

Yorkshire is the birthplace of the sculptor Henry Moore and the painter David Hockney, two of the world's most famous contemporary artists. Moore was born in Castleford in 1898 and first made his international reputation in 1948, when he won the Venice Biennale sculpture prize. His work, which can be seen in museums and art galleries all over the world, is well represented in Yorkshire. Moore, who died in 1986, was awarded the coveted Order of Merit for his contribution to the world of art. David Hockney was born in Bradford in 1937, and first studied at Bradford College of Art. Hockney is now famous not only for his paintings but also his stage designs and photography, and he occasionally returns to Bradford from his home in California.

Two of the most famous contemporary poets have Yorkshire connections. Ted Hughes, who was born at Mytholmroyd in 1930, has been described by Edward Lucie-Smith as 'the most explosively individual poetic talent to appear in England since the war'. A great influence on Hughes has been the millstone grit landscape of his birthplace. He became Poet Laureate in 1985. Philip Larkin, although not born in Yorkshire, spent most of his working life as Librarian at the University of Hull. Larkin's somewhat pessimistic view of life came to characterise much of the 1950s and 1960s and influenced many younger than himself. On his death in 1986 the country lost one of its finest poets.

Many successful attempts have been made to preserve and enrich the county's heritage, including that of the Industrial Revolution – though one of Yorkshire's finest writers, Bradford-born J. B. Priestley, was to decry the loss of many great buildings. The York Railway Museum commemorates the age of the steam train and the history of the woollen textile industry is remembered in several locations, notably in the Bradford Industrial Museum, which contains working examples of early textile machinery. Museums and art galleries abound and many old traditions have been revived, such as the York Mystery Plays which restarted in 1951.

Badge of the Yorkshire Archaeological Society

The county's theatrical and musical traditions have always remained strong. New theatres have been opened; the Leeds Playhouse, which dates from 1970, will occupy new enlarged premises in 1989, when it will be known as the 'West Yorkshire Playhouse in Leeds'. Old theatres, like the Bradford Alhambra, opened in 1914 by the pantomime impresario, Francis Laidler, have been refurbished and enlarged. Hull has a lively theatrical tradition, where the New Theatre contributed a great deal during the management of Peppino Santangelo during the 1940s and 1950s. Hull also has the Spring Street Theatre and more recently the Hull Truck Theatre Company has received national recognition.

Orchestras such the Hallé and the B. B. C. Symphony play to audiences in Leeds and Bradford and many quartets and choirs perform all over Yorkshire. Opera North is a professional opera company based in Leeds and is justly proud of its reputation.

Other art forms have also fourished. The prestigious National Museum of Film, Photography and Television, recently opened in Bradford, attracts thousands of visitors each year. The Yorkshire Sculpture Park at Bretton Hall was opened in 1977, the first of its kind in the country, and the International Print Biennale in Bradford continues to attract entrants from all over the world. Much of the funding of the arts in Yorkshire is provided by the Yorkshire Arts Association, based in Bradford, without which many arts organisations would cease to exist. Oriental Arts, based in Bradford, seeks to develop an interest and knowledge of Asian Arts – music, dance and poetry – throughout the region. Local and regional festivals – those held in Swaledale, Ryedale, Harrogate; the Ilkley Literature Festival and the York Early Music Festival are just a few of the ones held in Yorkshire – continue to prosper, drawing not only on traditional culture but often introducing new art forms to the people of Yorkshire.

Alhambra Theatre, Bradford

War memorial mural in Leeds University

XX Yorkshire Parliamentary Representation

Before the great reform of Parliament in 1832, Yorkshire, compared with, say, Wiltshire, had less than its fair share of members in the House of Commons. One of the many reasons for this was that, when Parliament began, much of Yorkshire, which later became densely-populated mining or manufacturing country, was desolate, scantily-peopled moorland. The allocation of Members of Parliament which was more or less just in 1625 had become shockingly out of proportion long before 1832.

Not only was the total number of Yorkshire members much below the county's fair share, but they were not equitably distributed within the shire. Tiny, ancient boroughs like Hedon and Boroughbridge had two members each, while great trading or manufacturing towns like Bradford and Sheffield were not represented at all. Up to 1822 Yorkshire had 30 members – two from each of 14 ancient towns; and two knights of the shire. (Yorkshire counted as only one shire, though the West Riding alone was larger than the next English county in point of size – Lincolnshire.) In 1822 the county was allocated two additional members for the shire, so that in 1832 York and Yorkshire had 32 members in all.

Yorkshire had sent up its two knights even before Simon de Montfort's time. York City sent its members to Simon's first Parliament in 1265. Several other boroughs were enfranchised before the end of Edward I's reign, though some of them allowed their representation to lapse, and recovered it only in Tudor times. In most medieval Parliaments the only Yorkshire members sitting were those for the county, and those for York, Hull and Scarborough. Pickering, Tickhill and Yarm appear as boroughs for a brief period in 1295; Ravenser for a short time after 1300; Doncaster and Whitby in 1337. Even in Tudor times Yorkshire felt a sense of grievance at its under-representation in Parliament. It is interesting to note that, among the demands of the Pilgrimage of Grace in 1536 (Chapter X), was the holding of a Parliament at York, with representation for Beverley, Pontefract, Richmond, Skipton and Wakefield. Within the next eighty years all these boroughs except Skipton and Wakefield were in fact enfranchised. Until the late 17th century, in theory at any rate, the king might enfranchise any borough he pleased. In Catholic and conservative Yorkshire, the Protestant Edward VI gave representation to only one new borough. His Catholic half-sister, Mary I, called up M.P.s from four – Thirsk, Ripon, Boroughbridge and Knaresborough. All these are set out on map 16.

Hedon did not return members regularly until Edward VI's reign, in 1547. Boroughbridge, Knaresborough, Ripon and Thirsk began regularly under Mary I in 1553; Aldborough in 1558; Beverley in 1559; Richmond in 1584 and Pontefract in 1621. The last Yorkshire boroughs to be re-enfranchised were Malton and Northallerton, both in 1640. In Cromwell's Parliaments of 1654 and 1656, the Ridings were given four or six members each and Leeds and Halifax each granted one. Richard Cromwell's Parliament of 1658 went back to the old scheme: two members for the county; two for each of the ancient boroughs (and none for Leeds and Halifax). The representation of Yorkshire, apart from the increase of two members in 1822, was made on this plan until the reformed Parliament, after the Act of 1832.

Apart from the county members, and those sitting for the towns of York and Hull, hardly one of the rest of the 32 Yorkshire members was honestly elected. Most of the Yorkshire boroughs were 'pocket boroughs', in the hands of local noblemen or gentlemen (their 'patrons'). In the boroughs where the patron chose only one member, bribery often decided the other, e.g. at Beverley, Pontefract and Scarborough. Other boroughs were 'rotten' ones, and would elect anyone who paid for the privilege. At Hedon, for example, anyone might be a member if he paid the 300 electors handsomely enough.

Aldborough and Boroughbridge, each with about 100 houses, were pocket boroughs of the Duke of Newcastle. Of Beverley's two members, one was chosen by Lord Yarborough. The Duke of Devonshire owned all 84 of the houses having voting rights at Knaresborough, and so, of course, he chose the members. Lord Fitzwilliam chose them at Malton; Lord Harewood chose the two members for Ripon. The Duke of Rutland and Lord Mulgrave each chose one at Scarborough, Sir Thomas Frankland both at Thirsk.

The ancient town of Kingston-upon-Hull and the City of York were too big either to be bribed or bullied. So in general the electors there (1,600 at Hull, 3,000 at York) could choose the candidates they thought likeliest to make good members. The county itself was much the largest constituency of England, with some 25,000 voters. It was far too big to be controlled by any patron, but the expense of fighting a Yorkshire election was so enormous that only a very rich man could afford to run. From 1742 to 1807 there were a dozen elections. Usually by agreement, in order to save expense, the Whigs chose one unopposed candidate, the Tories another. When the parties quarrelled in 1807 and fought the famous election of that year, the cost to the candidates was something like a quarter of a million pounds, equivalent to several million pounds of today's money. Allowing for the change in the value of money, the 1807 election cost more than a hundred times as much as that of 1983. Fortunately for themselves, the chief candidates in 1807, William Wilberforce and Edward Lascelles, were very rich men indeed.

Wilberforce anti-slavery badge

It was not without reason that for a long time before 1832 Yorkshire

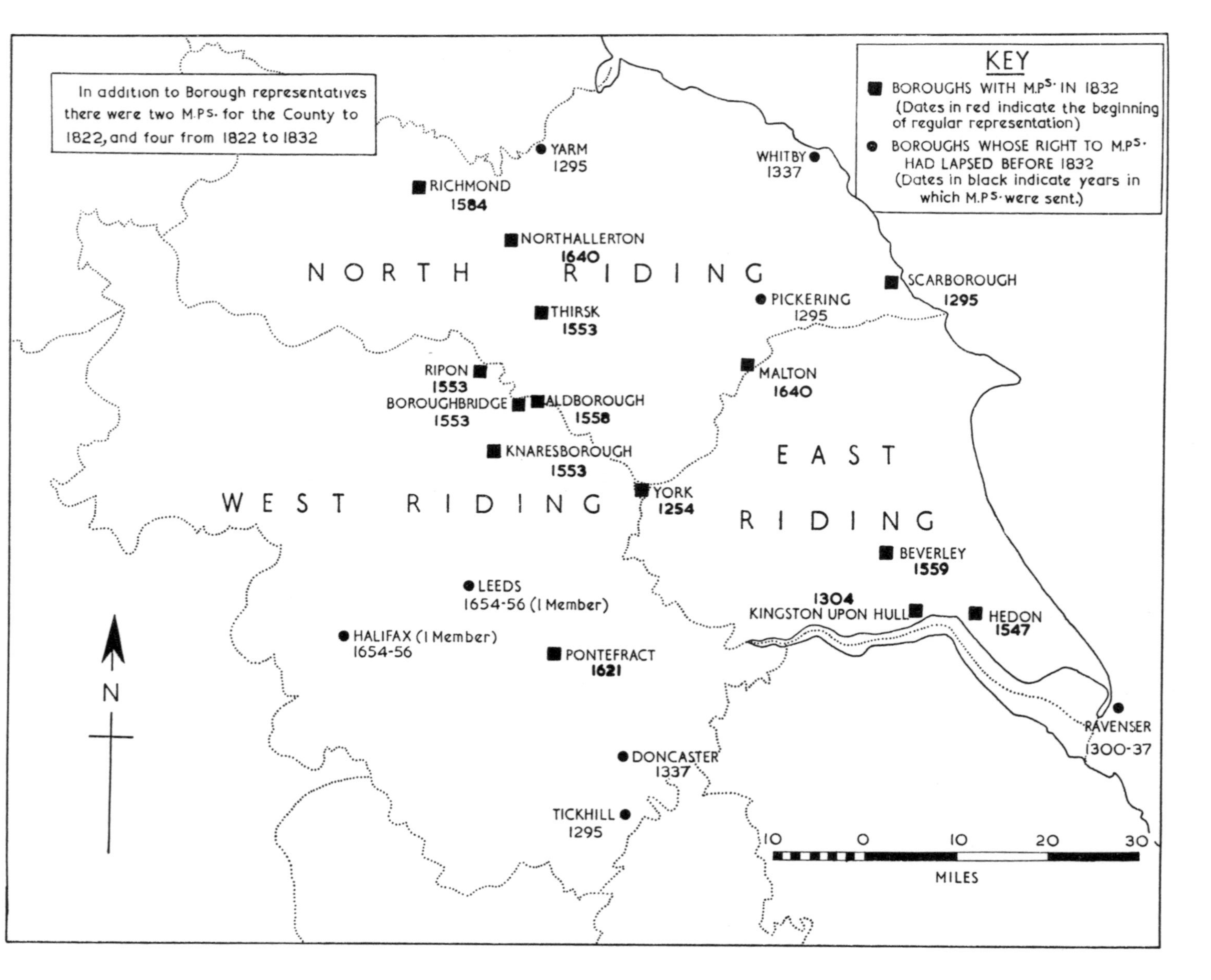

Map 16. Yorkshire Parliamentary Representation.

had been pressing for parliamentary reform, better election arrangements and a fairer distribution of parliamentary seats throughout the country. The great reform of Parliament in 1832 gave two members to each Riding, instead of four to the whole county. York kept its two members. In the West Riding, Aldborough and Boroughbridge each lost two; Knaresborough, Pontefract and Ripon kept their two; Leeds, Sheffield, Bradford and Halifax (which had not been represented before) gained two each; and Huddersfield and Wakefield each gained one. In the North Riding, two members were allotted to the whole area; Malton, Richmond and Scarborough each kept their two; Northallerton and Thirsk, which had had two, were reduced to one each. Whitby, formerly not represented, was now allotted one member. The East Riding was also given two members for the whole area; Hull kept its two; so did Beverley. Hedon lost its representation altogether.

Yorkshire was represented much more fairly after 1832 than before 1822. In a House of Commons of the same size (658), it had 37 members instead of 30 before 1822 and 32 between 1822 and 1832. The extra representation had gone almost entirely to the highly industrialised and densely populated West Riding. There were, of course, other reforms after 1832. These have affected the size and number of parliamentary constituencies and the composition of the electorate. There is now a regular review of the boundaries of constituencies. In recent years Yorkshire has always had over fifty members in a House of Commons which has varied in size since the Second World War from 625 to 640. Direct elections for the European Parliament were first held in 1979. In the second election, held in 1984, Yorkshire elected members for the following constituencies: Leeds, Sheffield, York, Yorkshire South, Yorkshire South West and Yorkshire West. There was also a member for the new county Humberside.

XXI The Map of Yorkshire

Arms of the East Riding

The external boundaries of Yorkshire remained virtually unchanged for over a thousand years, following the pattern established by the Danes in the ninth century, although from time to time during the succeeding centuries minor changes were made as some parishes were added or subtracted for the convenience of administrators, ecclesiastical authorities or powerful local magnates who had the ear of the monarch.

The name 'shire' pre-dates the Danish invasions, being derived from the Old English word 'scir', a division. In Domesday Book, Yorkshire was called *Eurvic Scire*, and associated with this already 'ancient' shire was an area known as Amounderness, which covered parts of what are now northern Lancashire and Cumbria. Yorkshire's connection with Amounderness was severed when Lancashire emerged as a separate unit in the 12th century.

The three great internal units, the Ridings, were also contained within the original division of the Danish Kingdom of York. The name Riding is derived from an old Norse word meaning a third part, and appears in Domesday Book as *Treding* (e.g. Est Treding, Nor Treding). The term Riding was in use in the 12th century, and remained as a modern administrative unit, but with deep historical roots, until the reorganisation of local government in 1974.

Within the Ridings the old Danish divisions (wapentakes) remained substantially within their original boundaries into the 20th century, although their administrative and judicial functions changed. In recent times some have retained only a vestige of their former importance as areas under the jurisdiction of a coroner's court. In the East Riding the older Anglo-Saxon term 'Hundred' was used, as was the case in most of England south of the Trent, where Scandinavian influence was less than in the north.

The pattern of local government which evolved to meet the changing needs of society during the period of dynamic growth and movement of the population from the 18th century onward resulted in many new administrative divisions of the county. This was particularly so with the boundaries of parliamentary constituencies, although at first it was difficult to change constituency boundaries because of vested interests deeply attached to the old dispensation, but this resistance was overcome by the Reform Act of 1832. Today there is a regular revision of parliamentary boundaries, and few constituencies in Yorkshire, even if they retain their original name, actually cover the same area as they did half a century ago.

There have been frequent changes in local government boundaries, none more radical than those which occurred in 1974 when the whole administrative map of the county was re-made. The Local Government Acts of 1888 and 1894 created a pattern of local administration which, whilst including the ancient boroughs and ridings, established new units such as urban districts, county boroughs and municipal boroughs. At the lowest level were the rural parishes, based on old ecclesiastical divisions which owed something to the 'vills' or townships of pre-Norman times and to the manors which emerged in the 11th century. The structure created in 1888 remained as the framework for local government until 1974, although there were of course boundary changes and changes of function.

The whole edifice was swept aside by an Act of Parliament in 1972, which came into operation in 1974. Under the old system Yorkshire had had 12 county boroughs of which the North Riding had one (Middlesbrough), the East Riding one (the City and County of Kingston-upon-Hull) and the West Riding 10, three of which, Leeds, Bradford and Sheffield, were cities with Lord Mayors, and one other, Wakefield, a city with a Mayor. The borough of Ripon, based on an ancient borough founded in A.D. 886, was also known as a city, although its local governent status was only that of a municipal borough.

There may have been some anomalies based on historical accidents in the style and nomenclature of some of the ancient boroughs, like Ripon in the West Riding, Richmond in the North Riding and Hedon in the East Riding, but on the whole these eccentricities did not greatly detract from their 20th-century functions, and may even have helped to sustain civic pride and a sense of community.

The 1974 reorganisation abolished the three Ridings and created several new types of local authority. The West Riding was dismembered and two new authorities, the Metropolitan Counties of West Yorkshire and South Yorkshire, were established. These were divided into Metropolitan Districts, based on the old County Boroughs, to which were added their neighbouring Municipal Borough and Urban and Rural Districts. In West Yorkshire the new Metropolitan Districts were based on Bradford, Leeds, Halifax (Calderdale), Huddersfield and Wakefield (Kirklees), Dewsbury and Wakefield. In South Yorkshire there were four new districts centred on Sheffield, Rotherham, Barnsley and Doncaster.

The boundaries of Yorkshire with its neighbouring counties were substantially altered. The East Riding lost Filey and Norton and the eastern half of the Vale of York to the new county of North Yorkshire. The rest of the East Riding, together with the Goole area, which were taken from the West Riding, was joined with the Isle of Axholme, and the North Riding area of Lincolnshire, including the steel town of Scunthorpe and the port of Grimsby, to form the county of Humberside.

Arms of the West Riding

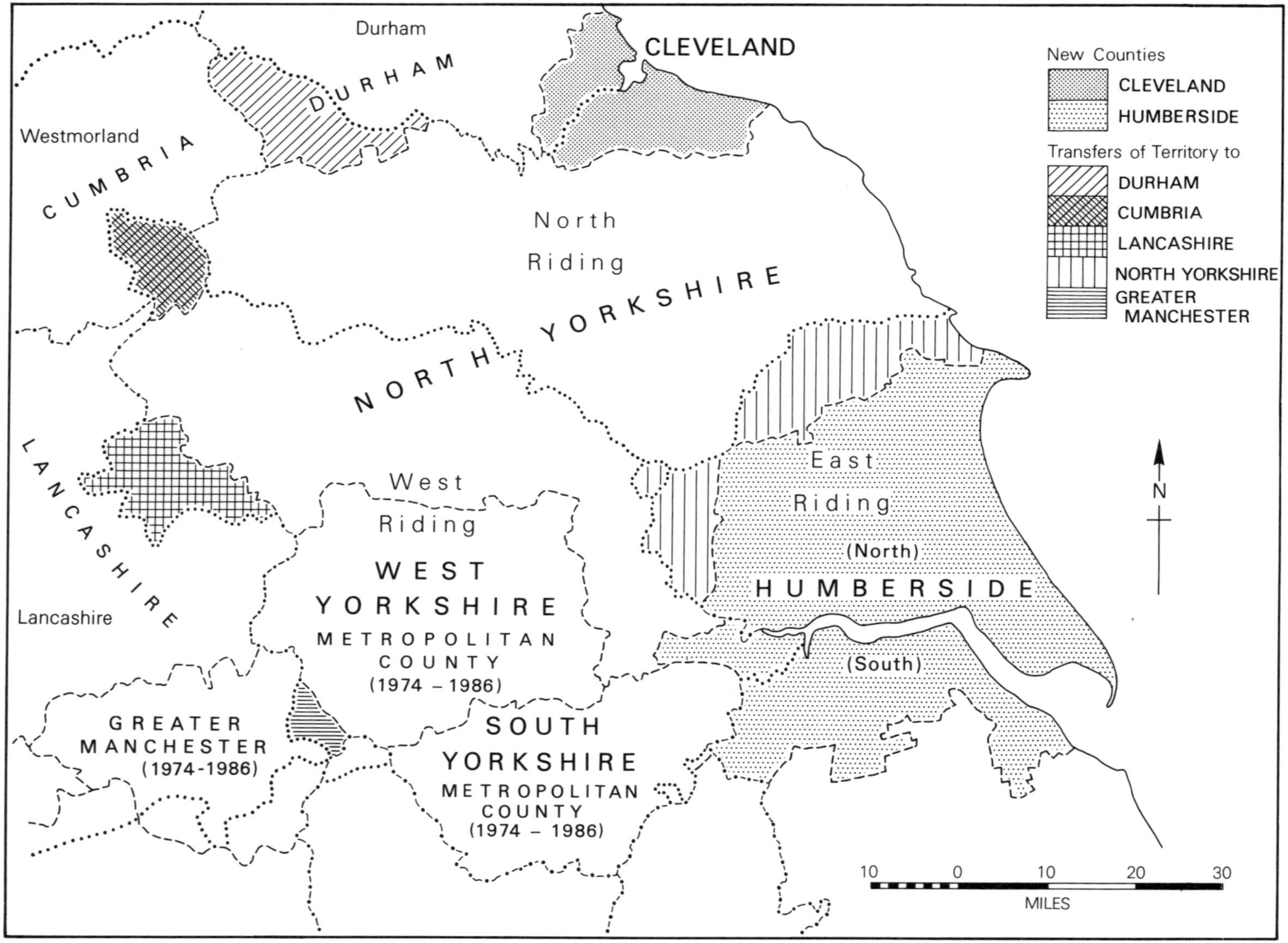

Map 17. Administrative Areas 1974-1986.

It was hoped that the construction of the Humber Bridge, completed in 1976, would knit North and South Humberside together into a viable economic, social and political unit. A similar riverside county was formed by joining Middlesbrough and adjacent areas of the North Riding to Hartlepool and other parts of South Durham, to create the county of Cleveland.

Arms of the North Riding

The North Riding also lost border areas in the west to Cumbria (Sedbergh), Lancashire (Bowland, Barnoldswick and Earby) and Greater Manchester (Saddleworth). What remained of the North Riding became the new county of North Yorkshire, to which was added a salient projecting south from York to take in Selby and part of the Yorkshire coalfield near Knottingley; and a large slice of rural Nidderdale and the mid-Pennines, from Harrogate to Settle. For reasons of administrative convenience the headquarters of North Yorkshire remained at Northallerton, of West Yorkshire at Wakefield. Barnsley became the centre for the government of South Yorkshire.

Barely ten years after the new arrangements had been implemented it was decided to abolish the Metropolitan Counties and redistribute their powers either to the Metropolitan Boroughs or to newly-constituted nominated boards. The other changes introduced in 1974, including the external boundary alterations, remain.

The redrawing of the administrative map is not the only change which has occurred to the outlines of Yorkshire over the millennium since the county was first delineated. The steady processes of nature, sometimes modified by human intervention, have wrought significant alterations to the shape of Yorkshire.

The Holderness coast between Flamborough Head and Spurn Point is slowly crumbling into the sea as the soft boulder clay cliffs disintegrate under the impact of the North Sea waves, and every year a little more land slips into the sea. Expensive public works have been undertaken, especially near the holiday resorts along the coast, during the last century, but they have only retarded rather than halted the inexorable advance of the sea. Since Roman times, a strip of land 35 miles long and between one and two miles wide has been lost. Houses, churches, farms and roads, have disappeared. Between Old Bridlington and Ravenser Odd some thirty lost villages have been recorded. Old Kilnsea, near the root of Spurn Point, is mentioned in Domesday Book and a church and a few houses stood there as recently as 1822. In 1831 the church tower was undermined and fell into the sea. By 1852 only the foundations of the church could be seen at low tide, and now there is no visible trace of them. At Owthorne near Withernsea the church steeple stood a cricket-pitch length from the cliff top in 1805, but in 1816 this toppled into the sea. Auburn, a few miles south of Bridlington, which some think may be the site of the deserted village in Goldsmith's poem which begins 'Sweet Auburn! Loveliest village of the plain', consisted of one ruined house in 1900, and today nothing remains. From time to

Flamborough lighthouse

time mile posts are dredged up from the sea bed. They cover the period from Roman times to the 18th century, and are evidence of former roadways, such as that which once formed part of the Beverley to Bridlington highway.

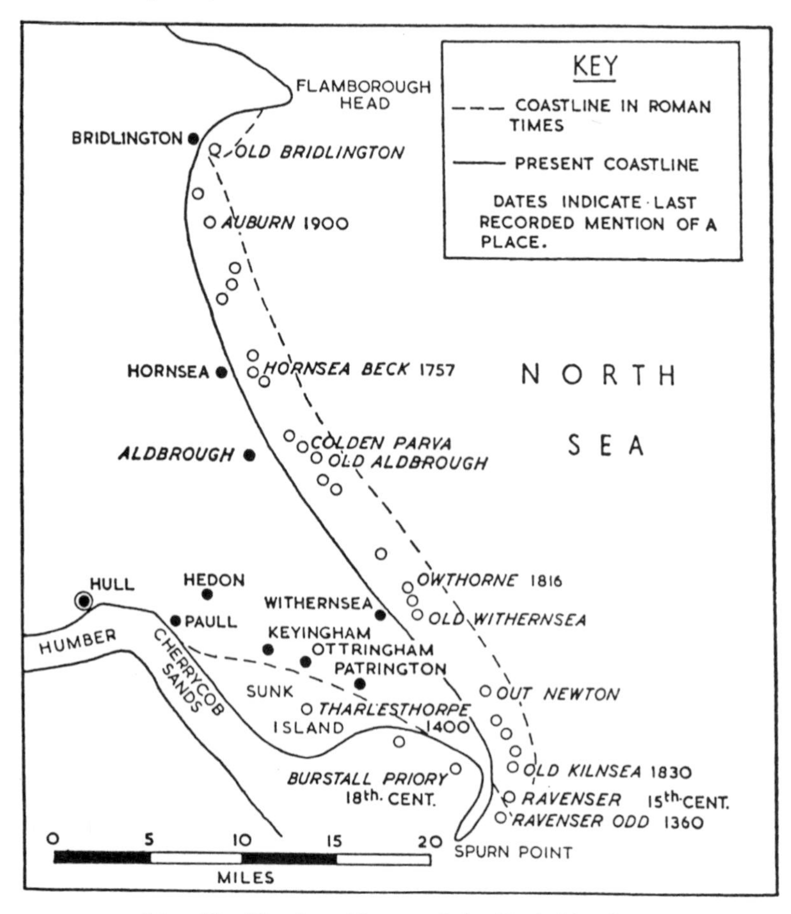

Map 18. The Lost Towns of the Yorkshire Coast.

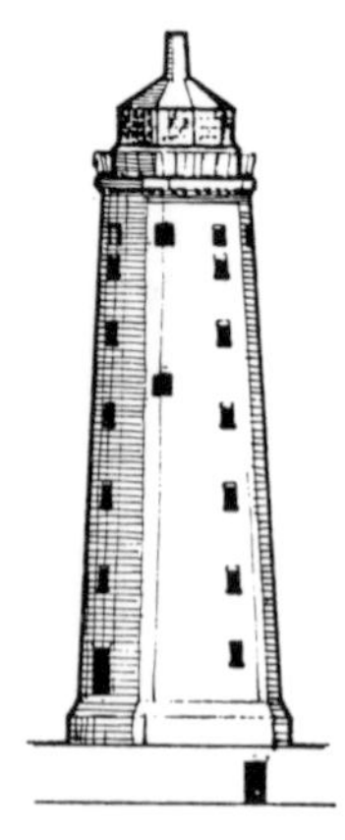

Spurn Point lighthouse

The material washed out from the cliffs is transported by tides and currents, much of it is redeposited in the mouth of the Humber, where it forms the three-and-a-half-mile spit of sand and shingle known as Spurn Head. The Spurn Head of today is two miles further inshore than the one which was recorded in 1066. Between these two are traces of two others, on one of which the seaport of Ravenser Odd flourished between 1235 and 1360, and on the other Richard Reedbarrowe 'Heremyte of the Chapell of our Lady and Seint Anne atte Ravensporne' built a lighthouse in 1428. The modern Spurn Head assumed approximately its present form about 1830. If past history is repeated, it should last about 250 years before it is cut in two by the sea, probably during a storm. The island thus created, on which stands the remains of John Smeaton's lighthouse built in 1776, will then be washed away, and Spurn will re-form itself further inland. This life cycle has been followed at least during the 900 years for which records are available.

The westward movement of Spurn created problems for ships navigating the entrance to the Humber, and the position of the lighthouse had to be changed from time to time. The ancient parliamentary borough of Ravenser was of greater size and importance than Hull in the 13th century, and for a time sent two members to parliament. Shakespeare mentions it as the place where Henry of Lancaster, later Henry IV, landed in 1399 during the Wars of the Roses.

If land is being lost to the sea along the coast, it is being won back from the Humber estuary both immediately inside the protective arm of Spurn, and also further inland along the north shore of the Humber. This is partly a natural process of deposition, but it can be assisted by human effort. The emerging bank of river silt and sand known as Sunk Island, a few miles upstream from Spurn, was mentioned in 1660 in the records of the East Riding Court of Sewers. Embankments were constructed to assist the work of nature and, in 1695, 12 acres had been reclaimed for farming. By 1668 it was important enough for the king to claim it as his property, and a century later 1,600 acres were under the plough. During the next century a further 7,500 acres were reclaimed. In the early 19th century Sunk Island was joined to the mainland, and to the nearby area called Cherry Cobb Sands. To maintain these large tracts of land in a good condition for farming, constant effort was required to consolidate the embankments and to keep the drains in good repair, but if this was done, the farmers were rewarded by the valuable agricultural land, which William Cobbett described in 1830 as amongst the richest and most fertile land to be seen anywhere in England. Here the farmer's gain has been the fisherman's and sailor's loss, as the growth of Sunk Island contributed to the silting up of the ports of Hedon and Patrington. Hull, which was once less important than Hedon, benefited because the deep water channel runs close to the site of the old port of Hull.

Similar reclamation work was carried out on the salt marshes and waterlogged clay lowlands at the southern end of the Vale of York, near the mouth of the river Derwent. Although some reclamation work had taken place in earlier centuries, even as far back as Norman times, the massive efforts made in the 18th century by the construction of drainage channels and protective embankments transformed the area from a marshy wilderness, where the boundary between land and water was indeterminate and fluctuating, into rich pasture land with grazing land for cattle and sheep, and fertile arable land growing wheat, root crops and vegetables. Defoe, writing in the early 18th century, described the Derwent as 'a river very full of water', which 'overflows its Banks and all Neighbouring Meadows, always after rain'.

Selby coat of arms

Another area where land which was once under water has been recovered for agriculture lies south of the Humber, between the Trent and the Don. Part of this is called Hatfield Chase. Here, in 1609, the Prince of Wales went hunting red deer, in a boat. The people of Thorne and Hatfield were fowlers and fishermen, living on patches of dry land among the fens and marshes. King Charles I was Lord of Hatfield Chase, an area of some 180,000 acres, largely marsh, extending into the counties of York, Lincoln, and Nottingham. He decided to drain the marshes, and called in the famous Dutch engineer, Cornelius Vermuyden. Vermuyden came over with scores of Dutch and French Protestants, who settled in the district and began the work of drainage. There are still a few French and Dutch surnames among the Yorkshiremen living in Hatfield Chase. At Sandtoft the strangers built a church which the local folk wrecked, because they objected to the changes in their way of life which were brought about by the work of the foreigners. Later engineers continued the work of Vermuyden (Chapter XVI), and in the 19th century many square miles of new land were brought into cultivation. By the method known as 'warping', a new soil was laid over the peaty moors, and the wastes of Charles I's time now produce rich crops.

The county of Yorkshire as we know it today is a creation of nature and society interacting over the millennium which has elapsed since the idea of a county called Yorkshire first emerged – and of course during the many millennia before the name was given. In the past, by trial and error, and often after disastrous mistakes, a fragile relationship has developed between society and the environment. The map of Yorkshire will change in the future as much as, or even more than, it has in the past; not only in the superficial pattern of administrative boundaries, but also in the more permanent changes which are wrought on the physical geography of the county. One can only hope that Yorkshire people learn how to co-operate with nature to improve the environment, rather than seek to dominate it in the interests of short-term gain.

AREA AND POPULATION OF THE NEW ADMINISTRATIVE UNITS

Name of Unit	Area	Population 1973(est.)	1981
West Yorkshire (Metropolitan) County	203,912 ha. (503,700 acres)	2,079,530	2,063,800
South Yorkshire (Metropolitan) County	156,049 ha. (385,400 acres)	1,319,180	1,310,500
North Yorkshire	830,865 ha. (2,011,600 acres)	644,830	684,700
North Humberside	234,366 ha. (579,118 acres)	551,130	560,900

Bibliography

It is impossible to give a complete bibliography of Yorkshire history within the space available in this book. The list below is merely a guide to further reading, with the emphasis on books which are likely to be of interest to the general reader and to be found in local libraries, although some reference works and more specialist studies are also included.

Bibliographies and guides to further reading

Elizabeth Exwood and R. W. Unwin, *Yorkshire Topography: a Guide to Historical Sources* (University of Leeds, 1974).
D. A. Kirby, *West Yorkshire: An Annotated Geographical Bibliography* (Huddersfield Polytechnic, 1976).
T. G. Manby, *Bibliography of Yorkshire: Prehistory to 1972* (Yorkshire Archaeological Society [hereafter Y.A.S.], 1973).
Yorkshire Cobook Group, *About Yorkshire: a Reading List* (1966).

Reference books and general histories

Victoria History of the County of York (*V.C.H.*): This monumental work began in 1907 with the publication of four general volumes and three North Riding 'topographical' volumes which appeared between 1907 and 1925. After the Second World War a second phase of publishing has resulted in *York* (1961) and *The East Riding* (Vols I to V 1969-1984). See also A. C. Price, *The County of the White Rose* (London and Hull, 1915).

Physical geography and geology

Geological Survey, British Regional Geology Series: W. Edwards and F. M. Trotter, *The Pennines and Adjacent Areas*; V. Wilson, *East Yorkshire and Lincolnshire*.
Cuchlaine M. King, *The Yorkshire Dales* (Geographical Association, Sheffield, 1960).
J. Lewin, *The Yorkshire Wolds* (University of Hull, 1969).
D. H. Rayner and J. E. Hemingway, *The Geology and Mineral Resources of Yorkshire* (Yorkshire Geological Society, Leeds, 1974).
A. Raistrick and J. L. Illingworth, *The Face of North-West Yorkshire* (Clapham, 1967).

Prehistory

F. and H. W. Elgee, *The Archeology of Yorkshire* (London, 1973).
A. Raistrick, *Prehistoric Yorkshire* (Clapham, 1964).
West Yorkshire Archeological Survey to A.D. 1500 (West Yorkshire Metropolitan Council, Wakefield, 1981), three vols.

Romans

Frank Elgee, *The Romans in Cleveland* (Middlesbrough, 1923).
Ivan Margary, *Roman Roads in Britain* (London, 1957).
A. Raistrick, *The Romans in Yorkshire* (Clapham, 1960).

Anglo-Saxons and Vikings

Anglo-Danish Viking Project, *The Vikings in England* (1981).
A. Raistrick, *Vikings, Angles and Danes in Yorkshire* (Clapham, 1966).

Normans

B. English, *The Lords of Holderness* (Oxford, 1979).
John Morris (gen. ed.), *Domesday Book: Yorkshire* (Chichester, 1986).
Trevor Rowley, *The Norman Heritage* (London, 1983).

The Middle Ages

See appropriate volumes of *V.C.H.*
J. L. Illingworth, *Yorkshire's Ruined Castles* (reprint 1938 edition, East Ardsley, 1970).

Yorkists and Lancastrians

F. W. Brooks, *The Council of the North* (Historical Association, 1966).
David Cook, *Lancastrians and Yorkists: The Wars of the Roses* (London, 1984).
William Hebden, *Yorkshire Battles* (Clapham, 1971).
R. R. Reid, *The King's Council in the North* (reprint, East Ardsley 1975).

Monasteries

K. Wilson, *Abbeys of Yorkshire* (Clapham, 1969).
Alan Philips, *Some Monasteries of Yorkshire* (H.M.S.O., 1973).
Joan and Bill Spence, *The Medieval Monasteries of Yorkshire* (Helmsley, 1981).

The Reformation

Hugh Aveling, *The Catholic Recusants of the West Riding* (Leeds Philosophical and Literary Society, 1963).
J. T. Cliffe, *Yorkshire Gentry from the Reformation to the Civil War* (London, 1969).
A. G. Dickens, *Lollards and Protestants in the Diocese of York* (Oxford, 1959).
M. Pocock, *The Tudors in Yorkshire* (Clapham, 1970).

The Civil War

Winifred Haward, *Yorkshire in the Civil War* (Clapham, 1971).
Peter Wenham, *The Great and Close Siege of York* (London, 1970)

The City of York

Alan Armstrong, *Stability and Change in an English County Town: (A Social Study of York 1800-51)* (Cambridge, 1974).
G. E. Aylmer and R. Cant, *History of York Minster* (Oxford, 1977).
Royal Commission on Historical Monuments (London, 1981), six vols.
Alberic Stacpoole (ed.), *The Noble City of York* (York, 1972).
See also the *V.C.H.* volume on York (1961).
York Archaeological Trust, *2,000 Years of York: the Archaeological Story* (York, 1979).

Agriculture

Board of Agriculture Reports, General Views: I. Leatham, *East Riding* (1794); J. Tuke, *North Riding* (1800); G. B. Rennie and others, *West Riding* (second ed., 1799).

W. Marshall, *Rural Economy of Yorkshire* (1788), two vols.
A. Young, *Northern Tour* (1770).
Bill Cowley, *Farming in Yorkshire* (Clapham, 1972).
W. H. Long, *Types of Farming in Yorkshire* (Leeds University): annual reports for several years after 1965.
W. H. Long, *Farm Life in a Yorkshire Dale* (Clapham, 1948).
W. H. Long, *A Survey of the Agriculture of Yorkshire* (Royal Agricultural Society, 1969).

The Industrial Revolution

John Ogden, *Yorkshire's River of Industry* (Lavenham, 1972).
Jack Reynolds, *The Great Paternalist: Titus Salt and the Growth of Nineteenth-Century Bradford* (London, 1983).
Fred Singleton, *Industrial Revolution in Yorkshire* (Clapham, 1970).
Michael Pocock, *A History of Yorkshire* (Clapham, 1978).

Roads

W. B. Crump, *Huddersfield Highways Down the Ages* (Tolson Museum, Huddersfield, 1949).
A. Raistrick, *Green Tracks on the Pennines* (Clapham, 1962).
K. A. Macmahon, *Roads and Turnpikes Trusts in Eastern Yorkshire* (East Yorkshire Local History Society [hereafter E.Y.L.H.S.], 1964).

Canals and navigations

Joyce Bellamy, *The Trade and Shipping of 19th-century Hull* (E.Y.L.H.S, 1971).
Baron F. Duckham, *The Yorkshire Ouse* (Newton Abbot, 1967).
Baron F. Duckam, *Inland Waterways of East Yorkshire, 1700-1900* (E.Y.L.H.S., 1973).
Charles Hadfield, *The Canals of Yorkshire and North East England* (Newton Abbot, 1973), two vols.

Railways

A Regional History of the Railways of Great Britain: vol. 8, David Joy, *South and West Yorkshire* (Newton Abbot, 1975).
K. A. Macmahon, *The Beginnings of the East Yorkshire Railways* (E.Y.L.H.S, 1953).
E. H. Fowkes, *Railway History and the Local Historian* (E.Y.L.H.S. 1963).
W. R. Mitchell and David Joy, *Settle-Carlisle Railway* (Clapham, 1966).
A. J. Peacock and David Joy, *George Hudson of York* (Clapham, 1971).
W. W. Tomlinson, *The North-Eastern Railway* (1914; reprinted Newton Abbot, 1967).

Post-industrial Yorkshire

Yorkshire and Humberside Economic Planning Council, *A Review of Yorkshire and Humberside* (H.M.S.O., 1966).
R. I. Hills, 'The General Strike in York, 1926' (*Borthwick Papers* no. 57, 1980).
Sidney Pollard and Colin Holmes (eds.), *Essays in the Economic and Social History of South Yorkshire* (Sheffield, 1976).
C. H. Lee, *Regional Economic Growth in the U.K. since the 1880s* (1971).
Alan R. Townsend, *The Impact of Recession* (1983).

Leisure and culture

Marie Hartley and Joan Ingleby, *A Dales Heritage* (Clapham, 1982).
Marie Hartley and Joan Ingleby, *Life and Traditions in the Yorkshire Dales* (London, 1968)
Robert W. Malcolmson, *Popular Recreation in English Society* (Cambridge, 1973)
David Hill, *In Turner's Footsteps: through the hills and dales of Northern England* (London, 1985).

Parliamentary representation

A. Gooder (ed.), *The Parliamentary Representation of the County of York, 1258-1832* (Y.A.S. Record Series, vols. 91 and 96, 1935-38).
G. R. Park, *Parliamentary Representation of Yorkshire from the earliest representative Parliament to 1886* (Hull, 1886).

The map of Yorkshire

G. de Boer, *A History of the Spurn Lighthouse* (E.Y.L.H.S. no. 24, 1968).
J. A. Sheppard, *The Draining of the Hull Valley* (E.Y.L.H.S. no. 23, 1967).
J. A. Sheppard, *The Draining of the Marshlands of the Vale of York* (E.Y.L.H.S. no. 20, 1960).
T. Sheppard, *The Lost Towns of the Yorkshire Coast* (Hull, 1972).
Central Office of Information, *Yorkshire and Humberside: Centre of Britain* (H.M.S.O., 1975).

Regional Studies I: The Yorkshire Dales

Amongst many books ranging from serious historical works to tourist guide books, we select the following: Marie Hartley and Joan Ingleby, *The Yorkshire Dales* (London, 1963).
M. W. Beresford and G. R. G. Jones, *Leeds and its Region* (Leeds, 1967).
Arthur Raistrick, *The West Riding of Yorkshire* (London, 1970).
Arthur Raistrick, *The Pennine Dales* (London, 1968).
B. Jennings (ed.), *A History of Nidderdale* (Huddersfield, 1967). (This is one of many local histories originating in adult education classes run by the Workers' Educational Association and University Extra Mural Departments.)

Regional Studies II: The East Riding

H. B. Browne, *The Story of the East Riding of Yorkshire* (Hull and London, 1912).
N. Pevsner (ed.), *The East Riding* (*Buildings of England*, 1972). (See also companion volumes for West and North Ridings).

Regional Studies III: The North Riding

Herbert Edlin, *North Yorkshire Forests* (Forestry Commission, 1963).
R. Fieldhouse and B. Jennings, *A History of Richmond and Swaledale* (Chichester, 1978).
O. Harland, *Yorkshire North Riding* (London, 1951).

Regional Studies IV: South Yorkshire

David Hey, *The Making of South Yorkshire* (Ashbourne, 1979).
Publications of local history societies, adult education groups, etc. are too numerous to list. Readers' attention is directed, however, to the excellent series of booklets produced by the East Yorkshire Local History Society, some of which are noted above.

Periodicals

The list of periodicals available range from scholarly publications such as the *The Yorkshire Archaeological Journal*, *Northern History* and *The Yorkshire Bulletin of Economic and Social Research*, to more modest journals such as *Industrial Past*, *Old West Riding*, *Victorian Yorkshire*.

Index